THE COMPLETE GUIDE TC

NORDIC WALKING

WITHDRAWN

D0858979

THE COMPLETE GUIDE TO

NORDIC WALKING

GILL STEWART

BLOOMSBURY

LONDON · NEW DELHI · NEW YORK · SYDNEY

Note
While every effort has been made to ensure that the content of this book is as technically accurate and as sound as possible, neither the author nor the publishers can accept responsibility for any injury or loss sustained as a result of the use of this material.

Published by Bloomsbury Publishing Plc
50 Bedford Square
London WC1B 3DP
www.bloomsbury.com

Bloomsbury is a trademark of Bloomsbury Publishing Plc

First edition 2014
Copyright © 2014 Gill Stewart

ISBN (print): 978-1-4081-8657-2
ISBN (ePdf): 978-1-4081-8658-9
ISBN (EPUB): 978-1-4081-8659-6

All rights reserved. No part of this publication may be reproduced in any form or by any means – graphic, electronic or mechanical, including photocopying, recording, taping or information storage and retrieval systems – without the prior permission in writing of the publishers.

Gill Stewart has asserted her rights under the Copyright, Design and Patents Act, 1988, to be identified as the author of this work.

A CIP catalogue record for this book is available from the British Library.

Acknowledgements
Cover photograph © Nordic Walking UK
Inside photographs by Kieron Lawlor and Peter Lay with the exception of those provided by the manufacturers of the equipment shown, especially Leki (including Figure 13.6 © C Schoech), and Figure 21.1: the cross-country skiing photo © Ernst Wukits; and the Nordic blading photo © T. Wenzler
Models: Lagle Moik and Jonathan Openshaw
Commissioned by Lisa Thomas
Design: James Watson
Typesetting and page layouts: Susan McIntyre

This book is produced using paper that is made from wood grown in managed, sustainable forests. It is natural, renewable and recyclable. The logging and manufacturing processes conform to the environmental regulations of the country of origin.

Typeset in 10.75 on 14pt Adobe Caslon

Printed and bound in China by Toppan Leefung Printing

10 9 8 7 6 5 4 3 2 1

CONTENTS

INTRODUCTION: WHAT IS NORDIC WALKING?

What is 'Nordic walking'? This is a question I have been asked probably more than a thousand times. My usual response is that it is an enhancement of ordinary walking that ensures that the whole body shares the workload, and in doing so benefits from every step you take.

It originally developed from the summer training regime of cross-country skiers. These days the techniques do not simply replicate that; they have been honed and simplified in order to provide an effective way to exercise outdoors. At Nordic Walking UK (NWUK), we compare the action to being on a cross-training machine in a gym, but the benefit is that you can do it pretty much anywhere, at any time.

Many people confuse Nordic walking with 'rambling' or 'trekking with poles', but both the poles and the techniques are very different. While both these activities utilise their poles for stability and also act to take some weight off the feet, only Nordic walkers use the poles for forward propulsion and exercise.

The best way to explain this difference is that a rambler will generally plant the poles into the ground almost vertically in front of him/her, while a Nordic walker will plant the poles at an angle and use them to gain a push forwards (replicating the pushing action that propels a cross-country skier along). This is impossible to achieve with normal trekking poles. Learning how to utilise not just the arms, but the massive power from the whole upper body, is therefore an important part of the process.

Many pole users believe that they are Nordic walking just because they use two poles, but this is not the case.

Case study: The converted rambler

I was once at an exhibition at which an elderly walker insisted that Nordic walking was simply branding and a way to cash in on something he had always done. I listened carefully to him and then asked him to show me how he used his trekking poles.

Off he went with good long strides, but he made a tapping motion with each pole, placing them on the ground in a fairly upright position in front of him as he took each step. Thankfully, he was using two poles and not just one as many people do, which involves an imbalanced action that can lead to one-sided muscular development and a twisting of the posture.

I complimented him on his fitness level and pace, and then asked him to shorten his stride and take smaller steps rather than striding forwards as he had previously been doing. When he complained that this was a waste of effort, I pointed out that his current arm action was not fully utilising his upper body due to the 'short' arm action and therefore actually wasting energy.

I made him aware that by doing this, he was using the full power of his legs, yet only two major upper-body muscles fully (the upper arm). His arm action was centred around the elbow and there was little activity in the shoulders or the rest of his upper body. This meant that he was not getting any extra power at all as much of his arm energy was going straight into the ground. This was clearly evident to me from both his posture and upper-body development.

After giving him a brief run-through of the Nordic walking technique I was able to demonstrate to the man that he had been wasting the energy from his arms and not engaging the larger body muscles effectively at all. By adopting our technique, he could also feel the forward propulsion and both the way in which his legs were working harder due to his increased stride and how his foot action was increased. He not only apologised for his earlier outburst, but also promptly bought a pair of Nordic walking poles. He also booked a course on technique.

In order to gain the full benefits of Nordic walking, you need to understand these differences and appreciate how to use the right muscles, plant the poles correctly and fully utilise the hand straps that are an *integral* part of the process. Once you have experienced the feelings of lightness, speed and power that can be gained through these actions, you will never look back.

However, like all other forms of exercise, Nordic walking needs to be adapted to your needs, in order to produce the results that you want. This book looks at the different ways in which Nordic walking can be used – for health, weight loss, fitness and fun, for example – and also explores how you can progress, while staying motivated.

Nordic walking inspires real passion among its devotees for the following reasons:

- It helps those who can't move well to move better.
- It encourages those who have forgotten how to move to enjoy moving again.
- It shows those who love to move how to do it in a balanced natural way that will avoid injury and develop an unsurpassed level of fitness.

Above all, Nordic walking simply makes you feel good.

PART **ONE**

1

GET STARTED

LEARNING THE BASICS

1

If you are impatient and just want to get started on your first Nordic walk, the basics are covered in this chapter.

Before you start, however, please read the following sections:

- For more information about poles or clothing see Chapter 9, pages 66–76.
- If you are looking for low-level exercise and want to learn quickly or have balance or grip issues, before you decide which method to follow see Chapter 2 on Exerstrider technique, pages 26–28.
- If you have any health issues or are not confident about your ability to exercise it is important to do the mini health check. See page 25.

YOUR FIRST NORDIC WALK

To begin Nordic walking, you will need:

- A pair of Nordic walking poles.
- Shoes or trainers with flexible soles and ideally waterproof.
- Comfortable clothing suitable for the weather on the day.

You can find more detailed information about them in Chapter 9, but as long as you have the basics you can get going.

It is always worth learning from an experienced, qualified instructor. No matter how much you practise, it's virtually impossible to ensure you are engaging the right muscles at the right time, unless you are walking in front of a huge mirror. Having an expert who can point out any faults and ensure that you are using the correct Nordic walking technique from the start is invaluable, although this book will guide you through the basic movements.

The basic movements will enable you to understand the technique, but you will benefit from going along to some lessons as well, in order to perfect your technique and also ensure that you get to experience the full potential of Nordic walking.

Before you begin any exercise, however, you should always warm up effectively (see Chapter 12).

HOW TO WALK EFFECTIVELY

It is important that before you even attempt to walk with poles, you make sure that you are getting the most out of every step when walking for fitness.

It's easy to fall into the trap of exaggerating movements when you begin walking as part of a fitness regime, and this can create difficulties when Nordic walking.

Rule one is to *always* remain *relaxed* and move *naturally*. Avoid tense, hunched shoulders, furious short-arm swings and stomping – all things that you see people commonly doing as they assume they are walking to get results.

If you follow these basic rules, you will feel your body enjoying the movement.

From the feet up, practise getting your body into **walk mode** and then go for a walk.

Walk mode

Stand up straight with both feet facing forwards, about a shoulder-width apart.

Focus on each area of your body from the feet up and do the following checks:

1. Make sure both your heels are aligned.
2. Align your hips; make sure one hip is not further forwards than the other.
3. Relax your buttock muscles.
4. Semi-engage your tummy muscles by tightening them just enough to draw the tummy button towards the spine. Do *not* over-tighten.
5. Concentrate on achieving a neutral pelvis position – which means you need to make sure you are not tilting it forwards or back.
6. Relax your arms and practise swinging them gently. They should bend gently at the elbow *after* they have started to swing

Look forwards with chin up

Hips aligned and natural pelvis position

Heels aligned

Figure 1.1 Walk mode starting posture

from the shoulder. This is called the '**double-pendulum effect**'. Bend them into a relaxed position with the hands pointing towards the centre of your body, not straight on – and remember to keep using this action when you start to walk.

7. Open the chest area by gently pulling your shoulders back.
8. Relax your hands and your shoulders. Make sure your shoulders are not hunched up by your ears.
9. Look ahead with your chin up, but make sure it is *not* jutting forwards.

Figure 1.2 The double-pendulum effect

Now you have completed the above checks, you are ready to start fitness walking. Follow the guidelines provided below to make the actual step movements correctly. It is important that you regularly go through the nine checks listed above. By doing this you can see if you have reverted to any bad habits once in motion. If that's the case, you will need to re-educate your body, but by memorising the checks and getting used to running through them until they become second nature to you, you can avoid this.

Foot strike

The first rule of effective walking is the foot strike.

Try to make sure that the heel hits the ground first, and that you consciously roll through the foot and push off from the toes. This will engage a lot more of your leg muscles and will also make you walk with better posture instantly.

Expert tip

Stand with one leg in front of the other and step forwards placing your foot flat on the ground, as if taking a step. Now do the same with the heel-first rolling motion of the foot strike, and feel how it uses more muscles and immediately feels better.

Practise walking this way while checking that the pelvis and tummy are all in the correct positions (see points 4–5, previous page). Now, you are ready for the next stage.

Bring your arms in. Remember to remain totally relaxed and perform the nine checks again to make sure your shoulders are not hunched and your arms are slightly bent, with your relaxed hands pointing to the centre line.

As you swing your arms forwards, make sure that you allow the swing to start from the shoulder and follow with the gentle bend of the elbow, hands pointing towards the middle. On the backswing take the arm past the hip. Note that this is a *fitness walking* arm swing and will be adapted later for use with the poles.

If you are completely new to exercise: Practise this fitness walking for at least a week, making sure each time that you perform the checks

Figure 1.3 The fitness walking arm swing with good backswing

above before you begin. Each time, try to go slightly further than the last time you walked. It's important to try to do both the warm-up and cool-down exercises from Chapter 12 before and after each walk. This will gently prepare your body and get you into the habit of exercise.

Expert tip

If you are particularly new to exercise, want to lose weight or relieve stress, you may also like to include 'mindful walking' and '4 × 4 breathing techniques' when out walking (see pages 54 and 155).

PICKING UP THE POLES

Now for the exciting part!

As soon as you grasp the propulsion element of Nordic walking, you will see how you can walk faster, further and more effectively than ever before. The method described in this section is designed to help you to instantly see, feel and understand the action. It will not, however, immediately make you an accomplished Nordic walker. As you work through this book, you will be able to decide whether you want to simply enjoy recreational results-based walking or move on to developing perfect technique, and therefore work on specific areas of your fitness.

Full Nordic walking technique is difficult to explain in one go, so we will begin with the 'NWUK 4-gear method' that is taught by instructors across the UK. In this section, however, we will only go through to Gear 3, which results in really effective, but achievable Nordic walking. Gear 4 and advanced drills are covered in the 'Improver' section (see Chapters 13–17).

So, to get to Gear 3, take your poles and let's get started.

Quick check before you start

- Are your poles the correct length and tightly adjusted?
- Do you have your straps on the right hands?
- Are the straps tight?
- Are the paws angled correctly?
- Have you warmed up?

You will now learn each important element required for Nordic walking. Each of these can be likened to a 'gear' in a car, and you will understand not only how to perform each action, but why it is needed. You will also be given drills to help you practise getting the gear absolutely right. Those of you who are impatient may want to skip the drills, but it really helps both your brain and your muscles if you perform them, and fully understand each and every movement.

GEAR 1

Purpose: Getting the power from your whole upper body with an effective arm swing. The sequence below is all about ensuring you learn to harness the power of the whole upper body by swinging the arms from the shoulder, not just walking with poles. Remember, Nordic walking originally evolved from cross-country skiing, and the emphasis is on powering yourself forwards.

PHASE 1: STEP AND SWING

Make sure you are unclipped from the poles and then pick them up by grasping the middle of the shaft with the tips pointing forwards as shown in Figure 1.4 (it's a good idea to put the paws on for safety, especially if other people are around). Walk around in a circle, remembering the effective walking checks (page 11) and drills, excluding the arm swing. That will gradually be adjusted for Nordic walking.

Concentrate on hitting the ground with your heel and rolling through to the toe, increasing the stride and achieving a good relaxed posture, as described on page 11. Using the poles to guide you, swing the arms from the shoulders so that the pole tips move forwards and back, but stay parallel to the ground.

Practice drill

Swing your arms and bend the elbow. You'll notice how the poles are heading *upwards* and

Figure 1.4 A correct arm swing will cause the poles to stay parallel to the ground

Figure 1.5 This drill will help you to identify incorrect arm swing

not *forwards*. Note also that your shoulders are doing *less work* because the action has transferred to the elbow.

Revert to the swing from the shoulder action, keeping the poles moving forwards rather than upwards. Once you have got used to this action, replace the fitness walking arm swing check with this one when Nordic walking (see 9 point posture checks above).

Concentrate on swinging the arm far enough forwards that the hand reaches 'handshake height' every time it swings forwards. You can either imagine you are reaching to shake hands or position your hand about level with your navel. Always make sure your upper arm is not held close to the side of your body as this means the shoulder is not working through its full range.

PHASE 2: DRAGGING THE POLES (OR BEING A 'FOUR-LIMBED CREATURE')

This phase is aimed at helping you to get the poles to the right angle for Nordic walking and that used for articulating the movement through the strap. Imagine that you have become a four-limbed animal and that you are going to power yourself along with your new long arms. The poles are now your lower arms; as you will not need two sets of elbows, keep the upper arm straight and assume that your *new* 'elbow' is centred around the hands and strap, and all the articulation is coming mainly from that point. The reason for this: if you bend your own elbows you will only use the power from the arm and not all the larger muscles in the upper body. The result of that is less power, and because you are using fewer muscles, you will burn fewer calories.

Practice drill

Start walking, as described above, with your hands in the Nordic straps, but not gripping the poles. Instead curl your fingers lightly around the poles. Remember to swing the arms as above, imagining that they are now longer with a joint at the straps. Keep your arm straight, but do not

Figure 1.6 'Dragging' poles, note the natural, relaxed curl fingers and forward hand at handshake height

tense it into a locked position; keep it relaxed but unused.

Drag the poles along as you walk. They should follow behind you (see Figure 1.6).

Concentrate on the poles for a moment. They should be bouncing along on the ground behind you, until your hand reaches handshake height. If the poles are adjusted to the correct height for you, they will feel as if they want to stop at that point.

Practice check: coordination

Because our natural rhythm is to swing the opposite arm to the leading leg when walking, you should naturally achieve this in the drills above. However, when people try to concentrate on coordination it often makes them stiffen and move unnaturally.

When you practise the dragging drill above, glance down at the leading leg and check that it's your *opposite* arm that has swung forwards.

Figure 1.7 Spotty dogging – leading arm and leg are on the same side

Figure 1.8 A tight grip causes the pole to be too upright and the arm to bend at the elbow

If they are the same side, you are doing what is called 'spotty dogging' (see page 147): you need to stop and go back to walking naturally and then swing the poles. Do *not* move on to other drills until you naturally fall into this pattern. If you are finding it hard to coordinate your arm and leading leg, see the common faults section in Chapter 16.

PHASE 3: GAINING CONTROL

This is where you start to really make use of your new long 'arms'. First you need to gain control of the poles. It is really important not to over-grip the pole, as this will make it stand upright.

All you need to do is cup the pole lightly with your third and little fingers (see Figure 1.9). This is more to stop the pole blowing sideways and tripping you up at this stage, although it it is also essential to help achieve a good Nordic walking technique in the longer term because this is where all the articulation will come from.

Figure 1.9 A loose grip with neutral wrist allows the pole to sit at the correct angle

Practice drill 1

Start by dragging the poles along, as you did in Phase 2. When you feel comfortable, gently cup the pole as previously described and then, when your hand reaches handshake height, allow the pole to slightly lift off from the ground, before you plant it back into the ground again. Be careful not to over-grip or change the angle of the pole in any way.

Repeat this a few times. Be aware of the pole biting the ground. Feel how you can lightly push yourself forwards with it in this position.

Practice check: are you gaining propulsion? (Pole/no-pole drill)

A good way to check if you have got this stage right is to get into a rhythm and then *stop* using the pole, but continue walking at the same pace. This should make you feel as if you have slowed down and are heavier on your feet. If you don't feel this, you need to go back through the whole sequence of dragging and gaining control and check you are not over-gripping the poles or bending at the elbow. Practice drill 2 will also help.

Practice drill 2: Trekking vs Nordic style

This drill will help you appreciate the idea of propulsion, which is the essence of Nordic walking.

Stand upright with your poles held as shown in Figure 1.11. Push down on the poles in that position, with bent arms, and feel how you go *upwards* and **not** *forwards*.

Imagine you have skis on your feet and ask the question: 'If I pushed on the poles in this position, would I move forwards?' The answer is clearly 'no'. Now try walking with your poles in that position and notice how only your arms are working. You have a shortened stride because your arms are leading the legs. This is *trekking* style.

Figure 1.10 Lifting poles to check if this reduces the feeling of propulsion and lightness on your feet

Figure 1.11 The arrow indicates the upward propulsion gained from straight poles

Figure 1.12 Light grip on the pole allows it to be used at the correct angle

Figure 1.13 Gear 1 – note the full swing from the shoulder and correct pole angle

Go back through the original sequence, until you reach the control stage. Push on the poles again as you walk. The lighter grip keeps the pole at the correct angle; note how this gives you propulsion forwards. Also note how your stride now increases because you have new 'long arms'. If you imagine the skis again, you know what the answer is to whether or not you would move forwards if you pushed on the poles.

Repeat this drill when walking by getting into Gear 1, and every now and then reverting to a straight pole and trekking style. See how, by doing this, it slows you down.

Gear 1: quick checks
- Heel-to-toe foot strike.
- Arm swing from the shoulder and upper arm, but not too close to the body.
- Opposite arms and legs.

- Handshake height.
- Loose grip.
- Pole angled backwards.
- Natural long stride.
- Propulsion.

GEAR 2

Purpose: Maximising the power gained from the poles.

Now you are in Gear 1 and can harness the power of your upper body, you need to learn how to get maximum power from the poles. This is where the straps come in, and why Nordic walking poles are so important.

Focus on the idea of your new long arms and how all articulation should be coming from the straps. So far you have only been holding the pole gently and giving it a slight push into the ground with a neutral wrist. Now, it's time to be aware of the straps and to use them to give you more power.

In order to achieve this, you will need to push harder into the strap with the outside edge of the hand once the pole has been planted. Be careful to keep your fingers cupping the pole, as before, at the start of the movement as you push into the strap. As you begin to add more power, the poles will provide more propulsion and you will increase your stride. As you push into the strap, you should also consciously push off more from your toes.

Figure 1.14 Maximising the power gained from using the strap correctly

Note: Remember Gear 1. Don't forget it because you're concentrating so hard on the straps. Keep your arm straight.

PRACTICE DRILL 1: UP AND DOWN THE GEARS

This drill is a simple way to feel the added power of the straps. Start from the beginning and get into your stride in Gear 1. Gradually increase the push into the straps; you'll notice that you speed up and stride out more. Drop back into Gear 1 for a few paces. Then repeat this several times. Notice how, as you add more power, you also increase the effort overall: you are beginning to use a lot of muscles and move faster than usual. It should feel good because the poles are helping you, but you will also notice your breathing quicken as you move into Gear 2. It's really quite simple:

more effort = more muscles = more calories

Therefore, every time you up the gears, you will be working a little harder.

PRACTICE DRILL 2: PUSHING OFF FROM THE TOES

Since you are using more power and speed, it is imperative to roll the foot from heel through to the toes. Consciously *push* off from the toes. Practice drill 2 is commonly used as a way to visualise this foot movement. Imagine that there is a lemon under your leading foot and that as you push into the strap on the opposite side, you push on to this fruit to squeeze all of the juice out of it.

Figure 1.15 Pushing off from the toes should replicate the action of squashing a lemon underfoot

Figure 1.16 Double-poling – the best way to practise using the straps effectively

Figure 1.17 Gear 2 – combining the correct arm swing with good use of the straps

PRACTICE DRILL 3: DOUBLE-POLING

This drill is a great way to really ensure you are using the straps correctly. Try moving forwards, but this time use *both* poles at the same time. If you have watched cross-country skiing, this action will look familiar. Feel how you have to use the strap to gain the power.

Now try double-poling *without* using the strap: simply grip the poles and see how you struggle to gain the same power.

Hopefully, you are now beginning to feel the action and are realising that it is not merely walking with poles, but using the poles to help your maximise the power from your upper and lower body in a natural movement.

This is the essence of Gear 2 – maintaining the forward swing to handshake height, but also utilising the strap to push you forwards.

Gear 2: quick checks

- Maintain Gear 1 arm swing.
- Squash the lemons.
- Push into the strap.
- Increase stride and speed.
- Stop pushing when arm is parallel with body.

GEAR 3

Purpose: Increasing upper-body engagement and workout effect.

This gear is where it really starts to feel like you are working. Therefore it's important to remember your goals and not to worry if you find it hard to stay in Gear 3 – that's pretty common. Think of it as something that needs practice. Learn how to switch it on and off. At the end of the day, if you want results, Gear 3 is going to get you them.

We have established how to harness the power from the shoulders and through the straps, but this gear is about pushing past the hip area, in order to gain even more power and to engage even more muscles.

It's quite easy to learn Gear 3 but less easy for a beginner to maintain it. This is simply because you are using even more muscle groups in this action. When we moved into Gear 2, we said we'd use more muscles used more calories. This is true, but in order for those muscles to work harder, they require oxygen and that is processed via the heart and lungs (see cardiovascular fitness and RPE on pages 126 and 142). They are like any other muscles in that they need to build up gradually and learn to cope with the added workload.

Note: If you start to feel breathless or uncomfortable at any time during these drills, drop back down to Gear 2 and build up to Gear 3 in short intervals.

Start by following the sequence of Gear 1 and Gear 2. When you feel ready, try pushing the strap further back, rather than stopping as the arm is parallel with the side of the body. To do this, you will need to slightly adapt your grip or you will feel awkward. Think of this as pushing the pole away from you. This increases the number of arm muscles involved and because the pole movement is longer, so will your stride be.

We usually allow people to master this by asking them to try pushing the pole further behind them and letting them naturally adapt the grip to compensate. Ninety per cent of people will relax their grip further as the pole passes the hip (see Figure 1.18).

Note that the hand opens, but the fingers remain in contact with the pole to avoid loss of control.

Figure 1.18 Pushing the pole past the hip

This should feel natural and seamless, so do not concentrate too much on the grip or it will become like coordination and detract from the important element of Gear 3 – that is, engaging the upper arm more and increasing the range of movement. Remember how the articulation was described as being transferred from your elbow to your hand in the strap? Now, you can hopefully see this happening and appreciate why you require Nordic walking poles.

You will know when you have mastered this action because you will both speed up and feel like you are working hard.

PRACTICE DRILL 1: UP THROUGH THE GEARS

As with Gear 2, the best way to fully understand each level is to build up from Gear 1 to Gear 3, and down again, making sure you fully understand the phases and also that you can feel the added power with each one. If you are finding it hard to stick in Gear 3, start by doing it in bursts (see intervals on page 124).

PRACTICE DRILL 2: ONE POLE ONLY

This drill is a great way to really concentrate on getting your pole use right, no matter which gear you are in. Put one pole under your arm (see Figure 1.19).

Run through Gears 1 to 3, making sure you complete all of the checks below. Concentrate on how the hand gently articulates from the light grip/control of the pole to the more open-handed push back. Think about the poles being your new 'long arms' and imagine the hand action in the strap is your new 'joint'.

Repeat using the other arm.

Note: One side of your body will always be weaker, and you will struggle at first to get the same control and solid plant of the pole on that side. This drill is a good method of working on that weaker side. It will soon build up with a bit of practice.

PRACTICE DRILL 3: POLES/NO POLES

This is actually one of the first drills you did. The difference is by now you will have learned how to really use your poles. This drill is therefore a good way to:
1. Make sure you are using the poles correctly.
2. Appreciate just how much propulsion can be gained by using poles correctly.

Figure 1.19 Gear 3, practice drill 2

Figure 1.20 Gear 3 – combining correct arm swing and strap use with a push past the hip

Get yourself into Gear 3. When you feel you are really powering along, lift the poles, but keep your legs moving at the same pace. You should feel deceleration and also very heavy on your feet. If not, go back through all the drills (see common faults in Chapter 16).

Expert tip

Try Practice drill 3 again on a nice steady hill. You will be shocked at how hard it feels without the aid of the poles. At this stage, we usually find people are not only convinced by Nordic walking, but also totally hooked on it.

Gear 3: checks

- Maintain Gear 1 arm swing and Gear 2 loose grip.
- Push past the hip.
- Articulate naturally with the strap.
- Feel increased arm engagement.
- Increase pace and stride to cope with larger arm movement.
- Note increased cardiovascular effort, but stay within your limits.

That's it. You now know the basics, and with a bit of practice you will be getting a lot out of your poles. You may notice, however, that if you are tackling a steep hill, you will find it necessary to adjust your pole positioning in order to remain comfortable. Below I have outlined basic hill techniques to help you when out and about in hilly areas.

UPHILL AND DOWNHILL TECHNIQUES

GOING UPHILL

On a fairly steep hill, when you are ascending, the ground is obviously higher in front of you and lower behind you. This tends to make planting in the way outlined above feel awkward and less efficient. There are a number of ways to combat this, depending on what you are trying to achieve.

1. If you want to maintain a good full-body workout the aim is to slightly lean into the hill, while being careful to maintain good posture (i.e. don't bend at the waist). Plant the pole further in front than you would do when walking on a flat terrain and slightly increase your stride length. The push back will be slightly shorter than when on flat terrain.

Figure 1.21 Nordic walking uphill

This method endeavours to share the workload and maintain a Nordic walking technique.

2. If you want to really engage your upper body while making the hill walk feel much easier, you could try the following adaptation that comes more from trekking pole use. Plant the poles out in front of you and use them to claw your way up the hill. This method transfers the effort to the upper body. This is good for reducing leg fatigue.

3. Finally, if you are taking on a lengthy, tough, uphill climb (walking in the mountains, for instance), you are likely to feel less inclined to maintain a full Nordic walking technique. However, you may find you can keep a slightly angled pole plant and gain propulsion from shortening your pole length slightly. While this is not ideal for undulating terrain, it can be a good compromise when tackling steep climbs. Trail runners use shorter poles in this manner to help them when traversing tough mountainous terrain and Nordic walking poles are ideal because they have the integral strap.

GOING DOWNHILL

Gaining propulsion downhill becomes less of an issue and in some cases totally unnecessary. The general advice in such instances is to use the poles to reduce the impact on the knees and provide stability. As the ground is rising up behind you, it's difficult to plant behind you. Plant the poles to the side of your body, with the tips just behind you, and adjust your weight so that it is on your heels when you plant your feet. Try to keep the weight away from the front of the foot by leaning back slightly and bending the knees slightly.

Figure 1.22 Nordic walking downhill

If knee pain is an issue for you, you may find it beneficial to keep your toes from facing directly downhill, too. By stepping sideways down a steep incline, you can reduce knee pain considerably. If the path is wide enough, you can actually zigzag down it. This helps to spread the load from leg to leg, although it does add a little bit of distance as well.

Expert tip

When trying out the uphill techniques, make sure you perform the pole–no pole drill (see page 22) regularly and it will prove to you just how much poles can aid hill walking.

PRE-EXERCISE HEALTH CHECK

Walking is a really safe way to exercise, and Nordic walking is a perfect progression for a beginner. That said, if you are new to exercise or have any health problems, it's best to have a quick health check before starting a new regime.

Below are some questions that may help assess your health level. This is not meant to be a comprehensive health check, by any means, but merely a way of highlighting issues that you should discuss further with your doctor or health professional before embarking on this programme.

MEDICAL CHECKS

- Have you ever been diagnosed with a heart condition or high blood pressure?
- Is there a history of heart problems in your immediate family?
- Do you suffer dizziness or chest pain when you exert yourself or exercise?
- Have you been diagnosed with a chronic bone condition (e.g. arthritis or osteoporosis)?
- Are you diabetic?
- Have you ever suffered from asthma?
- Have you been diagnosed with any other chronic condition that may affect your ability to exercise?
- Have you ever been told by a medical professional that you are obese?
- Have you got a body mass index (BMI) of more than 25?
- Are you expecting a baby or have you recently given birth?
- Have you ever suffered from/been diagnosed with an eating disorder?

LIFESTYLE CHECKS

- Have you been totally inactive for a long period of time (e.g. more than a year)?
- Have you ever smoked heavily?

If you answer 'yes' to any of these questions, please do not embark on the programme. Seek advice for a suitably qualified exercise professional. If you feel unwell, it is advisable to seek advice from your doctor.

Note: If you answer 'yes' to some of the checks, do not be put off. Nordic walking is an entirely suitable form of exercise in most instances. With the right guidance, you *will* be able to improve your health.

Once you have completed the above questions, it is advisable to get into the habit of performing the following **mini health check** before you set off on a Nordic walking session.

PRE-WALK: MINI HEALTH CHECK

- Have I eaten sensibly?
- Have I allowed my stomach enough time to digest the food?
- Have I drunk enough water today?
- Am I confident that none of my answers from the health/lifestyle check have changed?
- Am I confident that I have no injuries that could be compounded by exercising today?
- Am I feeling unwell and/or do I have a temperature?

EXERSTRIDER TECHNIQUE

2

USING STRAPLESS POLES

Some people find that using strapped poles when learning the Nordic walking technique involves a great deal more practice and concentration than they had originally envisaged. They want a far more simple, easy-to-learn method. The Exerstrider method is just that. It was devised by Tom Rutlin in the United States for use with his unique strapless poles. However, the technique's simplicity also makes it slightly less adaptable for use in some programmes (see the workout plans in Chapter 21) and for advanced techniques and sports-specific drills like those used in ski fitness (page 142).

If you are keen to take up pole walking and want it to be uncomplicated, while giving fast results, read this section before deciding on which poles to get started with. Exerstrider poles are also advisable for those people experiencing difficulty with balance or struggling with grip and articulation of the hands and wrists.

At Nordic Walking UK, Exerstrider strapless poles (see Chapter 9 on equipment, pages 66–76) are used for the well-being programme, Exerpoling circuits and work with fall prevention, active ageing and exercise referral patients. However,

Figure 2.1 The Exerstrider handle is clearly marked (left and right)

they are also used extensively around the world in a variety of adaptations by pole walking experts (e.g. see page 179).

This section outlines how Tom Rutlin himself teaches people to use his poles – in his own words – and this method is also available to view online (see www.exerstrider.org).

GETTING STARTED WITH EXERSTRIDER POLES

1. Select the correct height pole for you. The Exerstrider method requires the pole to be higher than that advised in the earlier technique section. To help users, the poles are not marked according to pole length, but according to the height of the user. This simple innovation alone creates ease of use.
2. Next, make sure that you have the left and right handles in the correct hands. In fact, they are clearly marked 'L' and 'R' and their ergonomic grip also makes them markedly different.
3. Stand upright and hold both poles with hands at handshake height in front of you.
4. Press down with both hands on the base section of the handle with the side of the hand, and concentrate on feeling the activation of the core muscles and upper body.
5. Next repeat this with a single hand, and note the diagonal nature of the muscular activation and increased engagement of the core muscles.

NOW IT'S TIME TO START MOVING.

The first stage in moving instruction is the 'transition'. In the 'transition', the poles are held loosely at one side, and you just begin to walk in your natural manner. Drag the poles, which are held loosely in the hands, and swing the arms in a relaxed, natural manner. Once you accomplish what should come automatically, you should begin to swing the arms further and further forwards until they rise to the handshake position. The landing of the pole creates a natural resistance. After this, while maintaining only a slight bend in the elbow, apply force to the poles; this helps begin propel the body forwards

Figure 2.2
Tom Rutlin

with each stride and the arms move in a pump handle action.

Tom says: '*I find this natural transition between normal walking and total body walking is all that is needed to get nearly 80 per cent of people "Exerstriding" but the steps below are used to remediate common problems some people have when their overactive minds prevent the body from moving in a natural contra-lateral gait.*'

If you do not feel coordinated or find it hard to achieve a natural rhythm straight away, try the following drills:

1. **The 'kick-start' technique** of initiating movement has the walker stepping out a natural, comfortable stride length with either foot, then holding the opposite arm in the handshake position, as the other hand loosely holds to pole. This naturally initiates a contra-lateral movement. If one does not sustain contra-lateral movement, then stop, get into the kick-start position and begin again.

2. **The 'march' or 'metronome' technique** is based on the rhythmic nature of natural walking. The feet strike the ground to the beat of a marching tune or metronome (tick-tock, tick-tock, and so on) and the poles land on the same beat. Generally, students should assume the kick-start position and then begin the movement using a marching tune or metronome to provide audible cues that are very helpful in maintaining a rhythm of both the pole plants and the foot strikes.

3. **The 'baby steps' exercise** is a remedial action for those who find even the march-metronome technique does not override the insistence that the mind, rather than the body's natural movement pattern, should be the guiding force. The student takes a baby step forwards with one foot, while utilising the opposing arm and pole. Then on the command 'baby step', they step forwards with the other foot, while raising the opposite pole and arm. The next command is not given until the last is completed. Gradually, the baby step command becomes faster and faster, and is alternated with 'longer step', 'longer arms' and 'baby step' until a gradual transition is made to a rhythmic contra-lateral gait.

The following drill, 'backseat driver', is one that is used by instructors to help people learn and understand the correct movements – it can also be performed as a partner drill.

4. **The 'backseat driver' drill** is designed to imprint a muscle memory of the correct/optimal range of motion of the arms. It is the responsibility of the partner to become an accomplished 'backseat driver'. That means being able to competently and consistently move the walker's arms through a proper range of motion as he/she holds one end of the poles and the backseat driver imprints a proper muscle memory of the desired range of motion of the arms. One begins by doing this while standing still. Once the walker and the backseat driver are both confident they have accomplished a desired range of motion, the exercise should also be done while walking a reasonable length of time (no less than 1 minute).

Note: Many NWUK instructors are also trained to teach the Exerstrider method, and they and their classes can be identified by the Nordic well-being icon on the website (www.nordicwalking.co.uk).

PART **TWO**

2

THE BENEFITS OF NORDIC WALKING

// WHY NORDIC WALK? 3

Nordic walking is quite unique as a form of exercise in that it provides benefits for everybody, from those with medical problems to the very fit. Whatever age, fitness level or goal, Nordic walking is suitable, effective and enjoyable, although it is advisable to carry out the mini health check on page 25 and to seek advice from a medical professional if you are in doubt as to your health and/or fitness level.

In this chapter, I have highlighted some of the basic advantages of Nordic walking over ordinary walking. Although most recent research tends to focus more on the applications of Nordic walking for the management of medical conditions such as diabetes and Parkinson's, it is important to examine the more general benefits. (See Chapters 18 and 19 for further discussion of fitness, health and research.)

GENERAL PHYSICAL BENEFITS

Nordic walking works within normal, natural movement patterns, making it a safe exercise for almost everybody. The natural exaggeration of shoulder swing combined with the push on the poles and a slightly longer stride all serve to help develop greater rotation of the spine. They also increase the general workload compared with ordinary walking. Use of the poles helps tone the upper body, while the greater stride and roll through the foot conditions the legs and buttocks. In short, if you are not a lover of exercise or you have little time to get fit, it is one of the best ways to ensure you target the whole body and get maximum results.

KEY AREAS THAT WILL SHOW IMPROVEMENT QUICKLY

- Posture improves noticeably after the first few sessions, and permanently with practice.
- Stomach/waist area is improved by combination of better posture and calories burned.
- The backs of the arms show more definition.
- Thighs and buttocks tone up.
- Ankle 'puffiness' is improved.
- Shoulders shape up and become more defined.
- General fitness and weight begin to noticeably improve after six weeks.

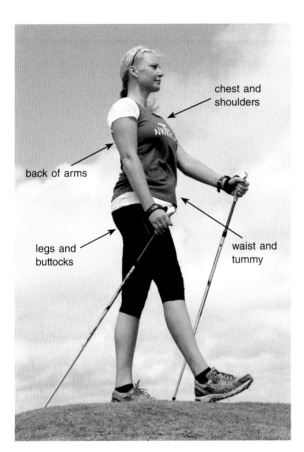

chest and shoulders

back of arms

legs and buttocks

waist and tummy

Figure 3.1 Key areas that show improvement after only a few weeks of Nordic walking

CARDIOVASCULAR AND CALORIE BURNING BENEFITS

Although it's impossible to truly measure accurately, there is a general consensus that Nordic walking uses 90 per cent of the body's skeletal muscles, a greater percentage than running, swimming or cycling. Almost all the large muscles that move our bodies are engaged at some point in the movement, and with Nordic walking being an upright activity, smaller muscle groups are also active in stabilising the skeleton against gravity.

Keypoint

Nordic walking works your upper and lower body. By engaging 90 per cent of your body's muscles (some people claim 95 per cent, if you're using facial muscles to talk to friends while doing it) it will tone your legs, buttocks, chest, shoulders and particularly the backs of your arms.

It's simple. Using more muscles requires more energy. Numerous studies have indicated an increased calorie burn with Nordic walking, the average increase being about 20 per cent more than ordinary walking. It is immediately clear when you are Nordic walking, however, that just how many more calories you use will depend on your Nordic walking technique; the better your technique, the more calories you are likely to burn. An increase of up to 40 per cent has been recorded, but for most beginners and recreational Nordic walkers, approximately 20 per cent is more realistic. As explained earlier (see pages 20–23), most people really notice the cardiovascular effect once they work in Gear 3 or add intensity, via hills or speed.

IT FEELS EASIER THAN ORDINARY WALKING

An often-reported benefit of Nordic walking is just how easy it feels – sometimes even easier than walking – and this encourages people to persist with it. Many studies have reported that participants have a higher heart rate when using poles and burn more calories, but when they are asked to judge how hard they are working many participants score it at the same level as walking

Nordic walking and me – some testimonials

'My first Nordic walk was about half a mile. After a year I can do a mile in 15 minutes and my average walks these days are between 5 and 10 miles.'

'I had a lesson in January so I could use the poles to help my walking with a damaged knee. I couldn't go far, only 100 metres at a guess; now I can do about 2km, slowly, and while it hurts a bit next day … the poles have been a life saver. I am also dieting and the walking has [helped] me shift over 9kg so far (loads more to go)'.

'I noticed my posture was better almost immediately. It toned my arms after about four weeks. I much prefer walking to jogging, there's no getting overly sweaty and you get to take in your surroundings much more.'

'I definitely felt a lift in my posture and my stomach muscles started to work; I also felt a difference in my arms and wrists. The fresh air is always a tonic regardless of whether it's rain or shine. All this gives me better sleep and relaxation. I try to do a little every day, but am not always successful. It is very necessary for my arthritic joints, knees and shoulders in particular. The poles give me added support, helping me to stride out with confidence. A great exercise.'

'After six sessions or so weight started to fall off (now 6.3kg in five months). Posture improved and walking in higher gears became the norm. I have now done my leaders' course. Keep walking.'

'It took me about four weeks to notice any physical changes; however, the feeling of well-being from being able to go outside was instant. A year down the line it's as if I'm a different person. The changes are still happening and will continue to do so as long as I can walk.'

normally. This is because the poles are literally aiding the walker: they tend to make participants feel lighter on their feet as the effort of moving forwards is shared between the upper and lower body. Poles encourage Nordic walkers to stride out and allow them to work at a higher intensity, without the discomfort typical of higher-intensity exercise.

Wearing a heart rate monitor can quickly reinforce this theory. Walk up a hill without poles and note down your heart rate. Next, walk up using poles in the Nordic style (at the same speed) and it will feel slightly easier. However, the heart rate monitor should indicate that you have actually worked harder (generally about 25–30 beats per minute faster).

IT TAKES PRESSURE OFF THE JOINTS

Many people also report that the feeling of being lighter on your feet provides massive benefits to those with sore knees or other lower-body joints. In fact, all the joints in the body will benefit from the fact that the load is being shared, but for beginners with painful knees and ankles, poles help massively, and allow them to build up meaningful miles. Often this also leads to weight loss, and that in turn eases joint pain – an all round solution.

IT INCREASES UPPER-BODY MUSCLE ENDURANCE

For out-of-condition and particularly older people, there is good evidence that regular Nordic walking can improve certain functions important to everyday life. It is extremely important to maintain upper-body mobility and strength, and to guard against falls as we age. Nordic walking ensures that the whole body is kept mobile and functional strength is maintained, thus making it easier to reach, lift, bend and move.

Nordic walking is an ideal exercise for older adults to maintain functional capacity and help them lead an active life for much longer than the norm (see page 43).

IT CAN DECREASE NECK AND SHOULDER TENSION

Nordic walking has been found to relieve neck and shoulder symptoms, and to reduce pain in office workers. This may be, in part, due to using the muscles of the shoulders in an action that encourages them to relax and drop down from their stress position (which is up by the ears), in conjunction with the better abdominal activity that comes from improved posture.

Keypoint

Get away from your desk. Nordic walking can be done in your lunch break. It doesn't require you to get too sweaty, and can help reduce aches and pains resulting from sitting in front of a computer.

IT HELPS TO MAINTAIN BACK STRENGTH

The slightly exaggerated forward arm swing in Nordic walking encourages a slight rotation of the trunk area that, when coupled with the longer stride and opposite rotation of the pelvis, results in greater spinal rotation. Spinal rotation and the resulting stresses that are placed on the inter-vertebral discs are important for the strength of the discs.

Nordic walking often elicits good muscular activity in the deeper layers of the abdominals and the pelvic floor. As the pole is planted and force applied through the upper body, the deeper abdominals 'brace' to maintain the skeleton's upright position.

Keypoint

Nordic walking is very effective at engaging the abdominal and pelvic floor muscles that provide core stability. It is an ideal way to take Pilates-style exercises outdoors.

PSYCHOLOGICAL BENEFITS

The mood-boosting effect of exercise has long been recognised, and physical activity has been used to help those with depression and anxiety for many years. More recently studies have shown that 'green exercise' (i.e. getting active while being exposed to or connecting with nature) has an even more powerful effect.

We all recognise that being in touch with nature makes us feel more relaxed and 'alive', while being active helps us focus the mind and combat stress. It's no surprise, therefore, that green exercise is now being used as a viable treatment for those in mental distress. The fact that Nordic walking is often practised in a group also aids the mind-boosting effects – exercise simply feels more enjoyable when you can share the experience and mix with others. Nordic walking is perfect for this because you still have enough breath left to chat with other people when in a group.

Other benefits of Nordic walking

In addition to the physical and psychological benefits of Nordic walking, there are other benefits, which are no less important:

- It can be done anywhere – no need for hills, country paths or snow.
- It appeals to all ages and fitness levels.
- There's no need to wear special exercise clothing.
- It's very sociable.
- It is easy to learn and to keep up.
- It's affordable.
- It's portable – poles can be taken to work, on holiday or even used as a way to travel.

Keypoint

Nordic walking is a perfect exercise activity, combining the mental health benefits of effective exercise with those of being outdoors.

If you're still not convinced, I would urge you to give it a go anyway. Over 90 per cent of people who attend NWUK taster sessions go on to register for 'Learn to Nordic Walk' courses because in a brief 45-minute taster they experience both the potential and the enjoyment that can be gained from such exercise.

Apart from the general benefits listed above, Nordic walking is also great for those with weight or health issues. The following chapters give more detailed information on how it can be used and why it is so effective.

NORDIC WALKING FOR HEALTH

4

Nordic walking is the most perfect form of whole-body exercise because it is gentle yet effective, and spreads the workload equally between the upper and lower body. Using the methods outlined in this book, it is also possible to build up the technique and movements gradually.

This chapter outlines why Nordic walking is ideal for certain types of medical conditions and whether there are any cautions you may need to be aware of. In most instances, if you suffer with any of the conditions covered below, it is advisable to take up Nordic walking under the guidance of a suitably qualified instructor (some conditions will require a Level 4 instructor, if in doubt contact NWUK).

JOINT, BONE AND MUSCULAR CONDITIONS

The fact that the load is spread over the whole body and you feel lighter on your feet makes Nordic walking fantastic for skeletal conditions, including arthritis, osteoporosis, joint replacements and weak or painful joints. It allows the participant to gain valuable fitness benefits without causing an overload on any specific area, especially the lower body.

With any joint problems there is a fine balance between no activity and too much activity, and it is vital to not overdo things in the early stages. However, being totally inactive may result in weight gain and stiffness, both of which are liable to cause more discomfort than gentle structured exercise.

The poles also provide support and help those experiencing weakness or pain to feel more stable, which in turn encourages increased mobility. For osteoporosis sufferers there is the added benefit of exposure to sunlight, a vital source of vitamin D, which helps with absorption of calcium and is essential for promotion of bone growth. The postural benefits of Nordic walking are equally important for this condition, and it can help to strengthen the most common fracture points: the hips, wrists and spine.

Joint pain can be a symptom of a number of conditions and once again Nordic walking can be an effective tool. Breast cancer patients, experiencing joint pain caused by their medication, have been enjoying Nordic walking as part of their rehabilitation at the Ladybird Unit at Poole Hospital, Dorset for several years.

Case study: Nordic walking and scoliosis

Amanda suffers from scoliosis (spinal curvature). An operation to insert a Harrington rod when she was 16 (now an obsolete form of treatment for the condition) has left her at nearly 50 with worn-out lower discs in her back and collapsed ankles. She discovered Nordic walking, and remarked immediately how the propulsion and lightness on her feet aided her movement and made her feel she was in control of the condition for the first time in her life. She is now able to walk taller and finds she can actually work on her fitness, rather than simply remaining inactive and in discomfort.

See also ankylosing spondylitis case study, page 162

CAUTIONS

Those with arthritis in the hands may find the strap interaction causes discomfort around the thumb joint and that the Exerstrider strapless poles are a more comfortable solution.

Exercise must be introduced gradually. Avoid the temptation to overdo it, even if it feels good.

CARDIOVASCULAR AND CIRCULATORY CONDITIONS

Nordic walking is an ideal exercise for those with high blood pressure, heart disease and other circulatory conditions because it increases oxygen consumption and heart rate but feels easier than walking (see page 126). This makes it feel less intimidating or fatiguing than traditional exercise, and yet more purposeful and effective than walking. The fact that it is fun and sociable also contributes to the level of benefit, because this makes it less stressful to take part in. In fact the relaxation gained both from being outdoors and the rhythmic action of Nordic walking can also encourage people to continue being active rather than viewing exercise as a chore.

The British Heart Foundation states that inactive people have almost double the risk of dying from coronary heart disease (CHD) compared with active people, and that one in five cases of CHD in developed countries is due to physical inactivity. Finding a suitable exercise activity is therefore really important.

Nordic walking does not involve a trip to the gym, the need to get changed or even becoming too hot and sweaty. It can also be incorporated into our daily lives. Most of all it can be fun. All of these factors make it the most perfect way to both prevent and recover from poor heart health.

For sufferers of intermittant claudication, a condition that causes pain in the lower legs when walking, Nordic walking has been found to enable them to walk further and without pain for longer.

CAUTIONS

Those on medication should always consult their doctor or exercise specialist as the medication may mask the physical response to exercise. Those with a history of coronary heart disease should also only exercise under the guidance of a medical specialist.

If you have hypertension (high blood pressure), it is important to ensure that your grip on the poles is light. Never over-grip the poles. Avoid tension in major muscles, especially in the shoulder area.

Case study: Nordic walking and heart disease

Bob had a heart attack at the end of 2011 and found that Nordic walking was an ideal form of exercise for his rehabilitation. He says:

'I first heard about Nordic walking when my cardio nurse mentioned it to me. I thought I'd give it a try and got a pair of poles. At first I could only manage a few hundred yards, but with encouragement from the team at NWUK I managed to increase the distance. I got to know what being outdoors was like again. I found parts of my home town that I never knew existed. I lost 38kg in weight and am now able to buy decent clothes again. Despite having a second heart attack in November 2012, I am still very active as a Nordic walker. In fact, because of my increased fitness level, I was back on my feet within a couple of weeks. My cardiologist loves my Nordic walking therapy. In short it has saved my life, improved my life and given me so much more than I could ever wish for. (Lost weight = less snoring = less thumps at night.) My son has recently started coming out with me, so for me it's a great package. I couldn't imagine life without Nordic walking now.'

BREATHING-RELATED CONDITIONS: ASTHMA AND CHRONIC OBSTRUCTIVE PULMONARY DISEASE

The main reason for using Nordic walking as therapy for those people suffering debilitating conditions is for maintaining or improving the ability to walk comfortably. It also helps to reduce breathlessness in general.

Because the poles and the technique enable you to add intensity to different areas (lower and upper body), Nordic walking helps improve breathing and lung function. The postural benefits of Nordic walking are, once again, significant for those with breathing problems as the poles and upright stance help to open up the chest.

Another bonus is that the poles provide stability and therefore boost confidence, as well as becoming a suitable 'resting post' for those needing to stop and catch their breath once in a while.

CAUTIONS

It is important to take at least 10–15 minutes of low-intensity exercise before increasing the intensity, and to include breathing exercises into your warm-up. Intervals are often more effective for chronic obstructive pulmonary disease (COPD) than a long period of exercise at the same rate of intensity.

Asthma sufferers should always take an inhaler and asthma attack card with them, and make sure others know how to deal with an attack. Be aware of cold weather and pollen; if they trigger your attacks, change the times you exercise outdoors accordingly. Check pollution levels by visiting www.airquality.co.uk and try to steer clear of busy roads.

NEUROLOGICAL CONDITIONS

Conditions such as Parkinson's disease (PD) and multiple sclerosis (MS) are progressive and affect people in different ways. Using poles in the early stages of these conditions (mild to moderate Parkinson's for instance) can help sufferers to maintain their general fitness and muscle tone. It also helps to encourage walking by providing stability. This, in turn, helps with confidence and energy levels. However, the benefits gained from the use of poles will vary from person to person depending on the severity and stage of the condition, and the specific areas affected. The response from groups working with both Parkinson's and MS patients has been excellent, and the findings of the first study into the benefits of Nordic walking on these conditions (by van Eijkeren *et al*. 2008; full reference on page 170) are also very positive:

'Compliance was excellent, and there were no adverse effects. These preliminary findings suggest that Nordic walking could provide a safe, effective, and enjoyable way to reduce physical inactivity in PD and to improve the quality of life. A large randomised clinical trial now appears justified.'

CAUTIONS

Slowness of movement, tremors and balance issues do increase the risk of falls, but this can be greatly reduced if the poles are planted further in front of the walker than advised in the technique section. Strapless Exerstrider poles help to minimise the risk of trips, but in a number of cases strapped poles have been used effectively, too (including in the case study below where the subject was adamant he wanted 'sporty looking poles').

TYPE 2 DIABETES

Research into suitable exercise solutions for those with type 2 diabetes shows that a combination of aerobic and resistance elements is the most beneficial. Nordic walking provides both within the same session. It also uses more muscles (at the same time) than many other forms of exercise, and is really effective for glycaemic control.

CAUTIONS

Those with diabetes should always keep a carbohydrate snack or sports drink (not sugar-free) if hypoglycaemia is a risk. It is also not recommended that you begin an exercise or activity session if your blood glucose levels are below 5.5mmol/l or above 13mmol/l and ketones are present in the urine (this can be tested by test strips), or if the presence of ketones is not known because no test has been taken.

OBESITY

One of the hardest things for somebody who is carrying a lot of excess weight is to begin to take more exercise. Often even walking can cause complications for lower-body joints and the feet, while other areas of the body can be uncomfortable due to chafing. In many cases, the discomfort will kick in before the exercise has provided enough results, and this often leads to a feeling of despondency. Nordic walking, on the contrary, provides a positive experience from the start, with the poles making walking feel easier and the walker feeling lighter on their feet. This leads to an immediate feeling of achievement because of the longer distances and duration of sessions that are recorded.

Case study: Nordic walking and Parkinson's disease

Kevin Howarth was diagnosed with Parkinson's disease in early 2004. He says:

'I was 54 years old (which means I was young as PD sufferers go). I was the head of a medium-sized comprehensive school in South Oxfordshire. My symptoms were bradykinesia (a loss of automatic response) and muscular rigidity on my left side. These effects combined meant I had developed a pronounced limp, which in turn meant I found walking tiring and tended to avoid it whenever possible. I was in a vicious circle.

By the start of 2005 I had taken early retirement and my wife and I resolved to travel as much as possible. When, in 2009, our good friends in Australia asked us to join them on their retirement trip to the Northern Territories, we jumped at the chance. However, as the trip approached, a nagging worry began to surface – how was I going to cope with the walking involved?

Fortunately for me another friend, who had been Nordic walking with NWUK instructor Jackie Gumme, knew of my worries. Barbara had a good knowledge of PD as her mother had the condition. Jackie had come across research that suggested the rhythms of Nordic walking were helpful to PD patients, who have a tendency to stumble and shuffle when they walk … I met Jackie in Windsor Great Park at the end of one of her classes and began to learn for myself. One of my difficulties was that when I walked my left arm just dangled – it would not swing. Well, walking with a pole made my arm swing. The more I walked the more subconscious the effort became and the more normal my gait.

Now came the test. In the McConnell Ranges, near Alice Springs, as I scrambled across broken ground towards a gap in the hills, I suddenly realised I was walking more steadily than my three companions. It really worked – I had achieved even more than I had set out to do. I remember sending a beautiful photo of the outback to Jackie to say thank you – you made this possible. I use my poles for exercise today and still find the benefit to be real. I am a lucky man.

Figure 3.2 The picture Kevin Howarth sent to thank his instructor when in Australia

Other benefits are the fact that there is no need to get changed or wear typical exercise clothing, and the outdoor sessions provide the opportunity to explore other factors, such as eating habits and self-esteem, in a relaxed, group environment.

CAUTIONS

It is important to introduce exercise gradually in order to reduce the risk of injury and discomfort. Supervised sessions that involve gradual progression and a variety of fitness elements will have the greatest results. Good footwear is of high importance, and should be comfortable, yet supportive. Some intervention to measure food intake is also important to avoid increased activity levels being cancelled out by an associated increase in appetite (see weight-loss plans, pages 44–46).

MENTAL HEALTH

The benefits of outdoor exercise on mental health are well documented, and Nordic walking is a perfect way to feel at one with your surroundings, breathe fresh air and take time out from a busy lifestyle or crowded mind. It offers other significant benefits too: the rhythmic action and need to synchronise steps can help encourage deeper breathing and focus the mind

Case study: Nordic walking and depression

Tony Dunne suffered from depression, anxiety and panic attacks so bad at times that he couldn't leave the house. He comments:

'With the help I received from Colchester MIND and the discovery of Nordic walking I now really have a positive outlook on life. I have just completed my fundraising for the London 2 Brighton 100km challenge that I Nordic walked on the 25 and 26 May 2013. I didn't break any records with a completion time of 28 hours and 49 minutes, but it was a fantastic personal achievement. I now have good mental and physical health and I know how important the help and support of others is to a life of well-being.'

on the activity. Also, the fact that new skills are being learned generally has a positive effect on walkers, especially when combined with the social interaction of group exercise. Nordic walking in a beautiful environment is extremely relaxing, and yet produces a sense of achievement and an energy boost. All these factors combined make it ideal for those suffering with depression or stress-related illness.

NORDIC WALKING FOR ACTIVE AGEING

5

Without wanting to strengthen the stereotype that Nordic walking is 'only for seniors', it is impossible to escape the fact that it is ideal for (and therefore extremely popular with) older generations.

This is not always as a result of the remedial elements of Nordic walking. There are many Nordic walkers, aged in their 70s and 80s, with fitness levels that the average 30-year-old would be proud of. Many of these people have led active lives (through running, trekking and other physical activities) and have discovered recently the whole-body effect of Nordic walking, particularly its positive effects on posture, ease of breathing and impact on ageing knees.

In this chapter I cover the functional elements of why Nordic walking is particularly good for older people. The previous chapter on health covered many medical conditions that are common in the elderly. This chapter, however, illustrates the importance of exercise as a preventative tool against illness, and also as a way to help older people remain independent for longer. If we do not remain active enough and ensure we incorporate the key elements of functional fitness (known as 'motor skills') in

our daily lives, we may start to lose the range of movements in our joints and gradually find our balance is not as good as it used to be, thus making us less able to look after ourselves.

KEY ELEMENTS INFLUENCING THE ABILITY TO PERFORM EVERYDAY TASKS AS WE GET OLDER
Strength

As we age, we begin to lose our lean muscle tissue and that not only means we become less efficient at using up the calories gained from food, but that we also lose muscle tone and, most importantly, strength.

A vital component in the fight to remain active and independent, maintaining strength is key to living a fit and healthy life. While walking is a fantastic way to ensure the muscles in the lower body and cardiovascular system remain in good shape, it does not engage the upper body sufficiently to stop those muscles becoming weak. Lack of use of the arm, chest and shoulder muscles will result in difficulties with reaching, lifting and even putting a coat on. In fact, seemingly 'fit' senior joggers can have particularly weak upper-body muscles that may pose a problem should they ever stumble and fall. Regular Nordic walking will use these vital muscles and a good instructor will also incorporate a few resistance exercises into a routine to boost everyday upper-body strength. Nordic walking will also benefit postural strength, and that has a positive impact in preventing falls and helping to ensure good breathing function as the chest area remains more 'open'.

Flexibility

Increased flexibility improves the range of movement of the joints and, quite simply, makes bending, reaching and everyday living more comfortable. It also prevents stiffness and relieves associated aches and pains. While Nordic walking – and exercise in general – will help prevent joints from becoming stiff due to lack of activity, it is important to *always* follow the guidelines in the warm-up and cool-down sections of this book (see pages 95–110), if you want to increase or maintain range of movement.

Balance

This key element of fitness is often the reason why older adults lose confidence in their ability to exercise. This is why Nordic walking is such an effective first intervention. By providing support, it encourages mobility and improved posture, which in turn help to strengthen the core and major muscles. Again, a good instructor will also encourage participants to perform balance drills when warming up and during sessions, such as well-being walks. The poles provide the perfect tools for such drills: the perfect progression is to reach the point where they can be performed without the aid of the poles.

Endurance

Simple cardiovascular exercise ensures that the whole body continues to function well, has a positive impact on weight, and reduces the risk of high blood pressure and poor heart health. It also aids sleep and helps fight fatigue. In fact, although many older people think they will feel 'tired out' after taking exercise, with Nordic walking the reverse is true and energy levels are generally increased. This is because the load is shared by the whole body and therefore no area is over-fatigued.

Brain function and mood

Exercise in general has been proven to keep the brain active. That in turn can prevent memory loss and even dementia. It is also widely believed that exercise may help slow down the progression of brain disorders, such as Alzheimer's disease. The repetitive coordination required when Nordic walking proves both relaxing and stimulating. This all has a positive impact on mood, especially as it is coupled with being outdoors in a sociable environment.

Expert tip

The advice from the Chief Medical Officer for the UK is quite clear:

- Older adults should undertake physical activity to improve muscle strength, at least two days a week.
- Older adults, at risk of falls, should incorporate physical activity to improve balance and coordination, at least two days a week.

WHY NORDIC WALKING IS SO IDEAL FOR OLDER PEOPLE

Perhaps the most important reason that Nordic walking is so good for active ageing is that it can be performed pretty much anywhere. Therefore, it does not need to involve the kinds of travel and entry costs required for a typical fitness session in a gym or centre. It is also easy to learn and does not require specific, possibly expensive clothing.

The social aspect of Nordic walking is also a major benefit to the people who undertake it. We often hear comments such as 'This does not feel like exercise at all' from those in groups where the main reason for attendance may be the chance to chat as they walk. By taking Nordic walking into a community, we can also break down barriers and help integrate people of different ages and cultures. This massively reduces the feelings of isolation often experienced by older adults, and can have a beneficial effect on mood and mental health.

One of the most inspirational Nordic walking projects I have personally witnessed was when an enlightened physical activity promotion team, Bucks and Milton Keynes Sports Partnership, trained senior members of the community to deliver Nordic walking to their peers. The result was not only a brilliant project for the senior population, but for the general population at large: one of those instructors was soon teaching everyone from young mums to scouts. It brought the whole community together and ensured that the older walkers not only remained active, but also felt a great sense of worth.

In summary: it's never too late to start exercising, and the simplest, most effective and enjoyable way to do this, in my opinion, is to join a Nordic walking group.

John Searle OBE on Nordic walking and its health benefits

'In the UK and the rest of the Western world we are being engulfed by a rising tide of ill health: obesity, type 2 diabetes, dementia, certain cancers, stroke and heart attacks remain major killers. It is true that we are all living much longer, but not healthily, as older people become increasingly dependent on health and social care. The cost of their care rises year on year and is becoming unsustainable. Governments are at a loss as to what to do. But the solution is straightforward. People need to be more active. Furthermore, the degree of activity needed to reduce the risk of many of these diseases, keep people healthy and promote a healthy and independent older age is actually quite small: 30 minutes of moderate intensity exercise five times a week. (Moderate intensity means exercising at a level where your breathing and heart rate increase but you can talk in sentences.)

'Nordic walking is ideal for this; indeed it is better. By incorporating the arms actively it increases the intensity of the activity and provides a work out for the upper body too. It has an added value for older people in that the poles compensate for the loss of balance and coordination, which is an inevitable part of being old and inactive. It is ideal for getting people active.'

John Searle OBE is former Chief Medical Officer for the Fitness Industry Association

NORDIC WALKING FOR WEIGHT LOSS

6

Nordic walking is one of the most perfect forms of exercise for somebody who is looking to lose weight.

For some people weight loss is far more complicated than the simple 'calories in minus calories out' equation and it would take a whole book to even begin to touch all the areas that need to be considered. Those with emotional issues or hormonal imbalance need extra medical/ expert support and advice, while anyone looking to drop a few pounds will need to watch what they are eating, too.

Below is a simple workout plan which, when coupled with healthy eating and a few key tips, should help you on your way.

HEALTHY EATING

If you are serious about losing weight and are not good at managing your diet, try creating a food diary, using an online weight management tool (such as Pete Cohen at www.weightlossguru. com or Fitbug at www.fitbug.com) or joining a slimming group. All of these actions may help you to stay on top of what you are consuming; these days such groups are really supportive and

their advice is fairly simple to follow. There is substantial evidence that those who write down what they consume or join an expert or social support network are more likely to succeed in losing or controlling their weight. Couple this with our plans below and you should soon start to feel livelier and notice some changes in your body as well.

EATING FOR WEIGHT LOSS

- Learn how to relax about losing weight – mindful walking (Chapter 17) is a great way to slow down and take care of your body, rather than constantly being unhappy with it. Being stressed encourages your body to store fats – so try to be patient and positive.
- Stay hydrated. Drink when you are thirsty and make sure you drink before you start eating. It may help you feel less hungry.
- Eat fresh, seasonal and local produce whenever you can and always aim for a good range of fruit and vegetables.
- Choose colourful, natural foods as these will boost your ability to ward off illness, as well as helping maintain a healthy weight.
- Try juicing in order to ensure your body gets

the vital nutrition that can help stave off hunger pangs and keep energy levels high. Be sure to include vegetables to avoid an overload of fruit sugars.

- Always eat breakfast, and make sure you eat well during the day and lighter meals in the evening.
- Balance your meals to ensure you have protein with every meal, along with healthy wholegrain carbohydrates and plenty of salad or veg. In the evenings, cut down on the carbohydrates if you can.
- Minimise or avoid processed foods, sugar, alcohol and caffeine as they are all 'habit forming'. Once you get used to enjoying them only occasionally, you will notice how you crave them less on a daily basis.
- One golden rule from Pete Cohen (known as the 'weight loss guru') is not to try and make too many changes at once. Take it easy and make gradual changes to your eating and activity levels. If you take your time and treat your body to a new way of living, you will feel great and want to continue forever.
- Some NWUK instructors do offer specific weight loss classes that include membership of the Pete Cohen plan. Others work closely with local slimming groups to offer exercise sessions that complement the activity advice given by the club.

EXERCISE FOR WEIGHT LOSS

- Whether you choose Nordic walking or not, exercise can be far more effective if you do not simply head out and do the same thing every day. The secret as far as weight loss is concerned is to mix it up. A skilled instructor will ensure that you are changing pace, performing drills and using techniques in a way that works on different elements of fitness and help you to target body fat.
- Slow, steady workouts, for instance, have long been advised for those losing weight. Yet recently, short, fast bursts of high-intensity exercise have also been proving popular.
- Avoid fads and anything that sounds too good to be true, and be sure to include the following into your weekly Nordic walking plan:
  - Include at least one longer, slow, steady-pace session and aim to increase this each week.
  - Include at least two shorter sessions where you vary the speed and intensity via the gears and drills.
  - Incorporate some form of resistance work (using weights to tone and improve muscles) into your plan, at least twice a week. This can be via bands, partner work or street furniture (see pages 127–141) – or if you prefer join a gym or use home equipment.
  - Remember to breathe deeply and not get so out of breath that you are gasping for air.
  - Allow yourself some time each week to simply enjoy your Nordic walk rather than constantly pushing, monitoring performance or focusing on the weight loss (try mindful walking – see page 54).
  - Stay hydrated at all times. Do not try to exercise unless you have eaten good balanced meals (ideally about 1.5 hours prior to starting) because your body will not run on empty.

SCALES VS MEASURING TAPE

One final thing to remember is not to rely solely on those scales.

If you have been Nordic walking, you will have encouraged your muscles to tone up and develop new lean tissue. This weighs more than fat, so it might cancel out any early weight loss on the scales, but if you measure your waist, you should start to see a big difference. Lean muscle tissue is like an efficient engine and as you begin to build it up it will also help you to consume calories more effectively. This is why changing the percentage of body fat and lean tissue on your body is one of the most positive things exercise will give you.

Once you have decided on some weight loss goals and started to make the changes mentioned above, check out the weight loss workout plans in Chapter 21.

PART **THREE**

3

WHAT'S NEXT?

WHERE TO WALK

7

There are millions of Nordic walking enthusiasts around the world and lots of ways to get out there and make the most of this exhilarating activity. This section looks at some of those that are available and gives you essential advice to help you stay safe and get the best results.

GOING SOLO

For some people, both exercise and walking in stunning scenery are things to enjoy on your own. Being outdoors and exercise are both great ways to unwind, and although it can be an extremely sociable experience, Nordic walking can also be a great way to escape from everything. However, there are a few things to think about if you want to be safe when Nordic walking alone.

Before setting out any Nordic walker should perform three basic mini checks:

1. **Mini health check:** Are you confident that you are not attempting something too strenuous for your level of health and fitness? (See page 25.)
2. **Mini skills check:** Do you possess the additional skills to be safe in the environment you are planning to walk in (hills, mountains, moors, for example)?

3. **Mini kit check:** Have you got the correct kit and refreshments for the duration and location of the walk?

These things may seem pretty self-explanatory, but even if you are a skilled outdoor enthusiast take a minute to read through the next few sections. It may make a difference.

ROUTE PLANNING

Even if you only plan to walk around the park for an hour, it's advisable to think it through and ideally let somebody know where you plan to go. This might seem extreme, but if you get into the habit of pre-planning routes, that will ensure you learn how to effectively manage things when you explore further afield.

Another benefit of pre-planning is that you can estimate the time it will take you to do your walk and avoid over-extending yourself by doing a longer walk than intended. Apart from potentially making you late for something, this can also lead to fatigue, which is not conducive to building up an enjoyable exercise routine. The guidance below is perhaps more relevant to walking further afield, but the same principles are worth bearing in mind whatever the duration of your walk.

The best way to pre-plan a route is either with a map, town plan or by using internet mapping. It's amazing how you can pick out paths you never knew existed and look at crucial things like how hilly the route is (this will add time). Other considerations may include:

- Is the parking secure and safe – if you are planning to drive there?
- Are there toilet facilities nearby?
- Is there anywhere to get food or water either during or at the end of the walk?
- Are there hazards, such as major roads, level crossings or rivers to be aware of?
- Is the terrain particularly remote or demanding? (Marshy, boggy, liable to be foggy, or close to cliff edges, for example.)
- Would emergency services be able to reach you in the event of an emergency?
- How would you contact specialist services, such as mountain rescue or the coastguard?

Mark out the route. When you attempt it for the first time, it's a good idea to check that you have mobile phone reception while out and about. It may be sensible not to walk regularly in areas with no mobile coverage.

It does also help to use tracking devices when first investigating suitable routes (see pages 88–91). These will store the route and allow you to track how much faster you are getting each time you walk it. A simple pedometer will track the steps and distance, too.

One final point when planning a route is to ensure that you have the right of way. Make sure you stick to designated paths or seek the owner's permission before walking on private land.

It is important to always understand the correct level of intensity of any exercise you are

Expert tip

In the event of an emergency anywhere in Europe – and also in over 80 countries worldwide – you can dial the European emergency number 112.

about to undertake. Make sure you understand your own body and learn to progress gradually rather than trying to do too much in the early stages. More information about getting the right intensity, understanding your levels of fitness and how to progress can be found in Chapter 14.

Staying safe on urban walks

Once out on a solo urban walk there are a few things to be aware of:

- Make sure pole tips are held away from other people, if you stop using them for any reason.
- Always carry ID (an NWUK Freedom Card will ensure people will know who you are, how to contact your next of kin and if you have any medical conditions).
- In crowded spaces your poles could be a trip hazard – be polite and aware.
- If you wear headphones make sure music is not so loud that it drowns out the sounds of a car approaching or a warning shout, for example.
- Avoid being alone in dark, secluded areas.
- Dogs on leads can trip you up, while those running free may be spooked by your poles. If they react, stop using the poles and hold them non-aggressively.
- In areas with traffic, wear bright or reflective clothing and walk face-on to traffic – except on blind corners when it's best to cross over briefly in order to be seen.

Figure 7.1 Urban Nordic walking

- Always carry a mobile phone, and check mobile reception and that it's charged.

Staying safe on country walks

- Make sure you *always* know your way back.
- Always carry ID (the NWUK Freedom Card will ensure people will know who you are, how to contact your next of kin and if you have any medical conditions).
- Watch out for uneven ground and hazards, such as rabbit holes.
- Be aware of animals. Stop using poles near horses and dogs. If they react stop using the poles and hold them non-aggressively.
- Be aware of localised risks, such as snakes, spiders or bulls.
- Avoid tick bites by covering lower legs when walking in bracken. They can carry Lyme disease, which is a bacterial infection that can lead to extreme joint and muscle pain.
- Be aware that mountain bikers, runners and horse riders may be sharing the paths with

you, and that your poles may make it tricky for them to get past.
- If walking on roads, wear bright or reflective clothing and walk face-on to traffic, except on blind corners when it's best to cross over briefly in order to be seen.
- If climbing over stiles or unlocking gates, it's advisable to remove one pole from the straps to allow full hand movement and avoid poking anyone in the eye with the end of your pole.

Expert tip

Always carry ID. If you are on medication that could affect treatment in the event of an emergency make sure you make a note of that and your next of kin in whatever you carry. The NWUK Freedom Card, for example, will contain a unique number that provides access to this confidential information via a secure server, should an accident occur.

Figure 7.2 Freedom Cards provide good ID for Nordic walkers

Respect the environment

Nordic walking is growing in popularity and we want to ensure that we are always welcome. Make sure you respect the areas you walk in so they remain available for all of us to enjoy in the future. To help do this:

- Know your countryside code and respect the environment at all times.
- Never trespass.
- Consider and protect wildlife at all times.
- Ensure you check that pole use is allowed and put paws on if erosion of paths is an issue.

Watch the weather

Nordic walking is suitable for summer or winter weather and we certainly never let rain put us off. However, I do advise that you check the daily forecast before you head out because you need to be properly prepared. There are two weather extremes that could make Nordic walking risky, but if you are prepared you should be fine.

1. **Thunderstorms:** Lightning is a risk to Nordic walkers. It is advisable not use Nordic walking poles during a storm because, like golf clubs, they could conduct electricity.
2. **Ice:** You can Nordic walk in soft snow, but very icy pavements or roads can be lethal. If there are patches of ice or packed snow, you should consider ice cleats (see the following chapter on equipment), otherwise steer clear until the ice has thawed.

If you are lucky enough to have hot and sunny weather, make sure you have sunscreen, a hat and some sunglasses with you. Carry plenty of water to avoid dehydration. Weather also affects air quality and pollen levels (see page 37).

Figure 7.3 Ice cleats

FITTING NORDIC WALKING INTO YOUR LIFE

These days, we are all so busy and it is easy to let an exercise regime slide as soon as it becomes difficult to fit it into your routine. Nordic walking is one of the most versatile forms of exercise and, once you have the hang of it, there are really no excuses because the poles take up no room, are a method of transport and you only need 20–30 minutes in which to get a really good workout.

Tips to help you fit Nordic walking into your life

- Encourage family members to join you. You are less likely to feel you should be at home with them that way.
- Get into a routine. Think of your Nordic walk as something that is as essential as brushing your teeth. Don't cancel it lightly.
- Ditch the car. Think about trips that you currently do by car and how you could replace

51

them with a Nordic walk. It is a great way to save on fuel and parking costs as well as get fit and avoid the stresses of parking. Obviously it is not ideal for a supermarket shop but taking the kids to school or getting to and from work is a great way to fit in a daily workout.

- Encourage colleagues to join you at lunchtime. A 20-minute blast with your poles will burn up calories and leave you feeling energised. The poles are easy to store and you need not get too sweaty, if you go at a moderate pace. Some organisations have regular Nordic walking sessions and even host Nordic walking meetings.

STAYING MOTIVATED

With any activity or new regime, staying motivated is the key to success and it can be a challenge for those of us with busy lives. The key to adherence in most cases is simple: if people are getting results, having fun and feeling good, they are more likely to continue.

I believe that Nordic walking is one of the most motivating ways to be active because it provides all of the above in a short space of time. However, you may experience periods where you feel less motivated.

Tips to keep you motivated

- Try to find a Nordic walking partner who will tempt you when you don't feel like it and may also encourage you to work harder on those lazy days.
- Some people find music really motivating, but some studies show that it can actually lower the feeling of effort. Using headphones will also heighten the risk of not hearing what is

going on around you and negate the pleasure of being out among birds and wildlife.

- Enter an event or challenge that will give you a goal to train for and possibly raise funds for a good cause.
- Have a mantra. Set a goal and keep repeating it to yourself if motivation drops. For example, 'I will complete the 10K walking race I have entered' or 'I will fit into that new outfit in six weeks time'.
- Add variety, drills and progression to your routes and sessions (see Part Five of this book).
- Keep a training diary in order to track your progress and help you to notice when things are sliding (see box below).
- Use a heart rate monitor, pedometer or route/ fitness tracking device (see pages 88–91).

What to include in a training diary

- Session type – e.g. moderate walk
- Time of day
- Distance covered
- Time taken
- Weather on the day
- Type of terrain
- What you ate prior to the walk
- How it felt or RPE (see page 126)

It can also help if you make notes such as whether there were any particularly negative/positive things about the walk, or who you were with. All of this information will help you to build up a picture of how you are doing and what works for you.

WHERE TO NORDIC WALK

Most towns and cities have lovely urban parks, but there are also some other brilliant walking venues that are managed by specialist or local organisations that actively encourage you to explore their beautiful and often historic outdoor spaces.

Many also have marked walking routes where you can follow a route map and even take advantage of walks graded by difficulty, time and distance. Your local tourist information office or library will have information about these, but I have compiled a list of useful websites to help you locate those nearest to where you may want to go Nordic walking.

Most countries also have national parks or countryside management areas. Here in the UK, there are a number of organisations that welcome visitors to outstanding outdoor locations.

- **The National Trust:** This has over 300 historic buildings, many of which are set in stunning parkland, gardens or wild landscapes which the Trust are keen for you to enjoy. They actively encourage walking and many of the larger estates have linked up with their local NWUK instructors to deliver Nordic walking courses and sessions. (See www.nationaltrust. org.uk/visit/activities/walking)

- **English Heritage:** This also manages sites with special historic interest and it also encourages people to be active in them, where appropriate. Some even have links with local NWUK instructors and promote courses on Nordic walking. (See www.english-heritage. org.uk)

- **National Parks:** There are 15 National Parks in the UK. The National Parks each have their own websites, containing information about how you can explore them on foot. These parks cover the most extraordinary areas of the UK and the opportunities for Nordic walking are numerous so please do check them out. It may be possible to find local instructors with the skills and local knowledge to make your visit even more memorable. (See www. nationalparks.gov.uk)

- **National Trails:** There are 15 of these long-distance trails in England and Wales, totalling about 4,023m, in addition to a further 4 in Scotland. The trails have been developed by linking traditional footpaths, bridleways and byways with newly created walkways. They include: Offa's Dyke (along the English/Welsh border); Hadrian's Wall (stetching from the Solway Coast in Cumbria to Wallsend near Newcastle upon Tyne); the South West Coastal Path (running from Minehead in Somerset, along the coasts of Devon and Cornwall, to Poole Harbour in Dorset); and the Cotswold Way. All of these are perfect if you are looking for marked routes for your Nordic walking excursions. They also provide great challenges for people who often undertake to walk them for charity or in order to compete against peer Nordic walkers. (See www.nationaltrail.co.uk)

- **Forestry Commission:** This is the government department responsible for the protection and expansion of forests and woodlands in England and Scotland. Natural Resources Wales is responsible for those in Wales. It welcomes walkers and it provides, in many cases, specific marked trails that you can follow. (See www. forestry.gov.uk/forestry/INFD-8XDGTK)

- **Canals and Rivers Trust:** This organisation is responsible for the management of the UK's waterways and has a number of stunning walking routes for you to explore. These range from historic inner city canals to meandering water meadows. (See canalrivertrust.org.uk/see-and-do/routes)

Other useful walking websites

- **Walk for Life:** This website has a great walk finder tool that enables you to search for routes in the areas you wish to visit. It also allows you to plot your own walks for others to go and try. (See www.walk4life.info)
- **Walking World:** If you want to find comprehensive notes detailing walks right across the UK, check out this website, which is a rich resource for walk leaders and enthusiasts. (See www.walkingworld.com/home.aspx)
- **Walk It:** Even if you are based in more urban areas there are plenty of resources to help you find great places to walk. (See http://walkit.com)

- **Ramblers:** Not specifically aimed at the Nordic walker is The Ramblers. It's a great resource with tips, advice and information on local walking groups. (See www.ramblers.org.uk)
- **Long Distance Walkers Association:** Another walking-based organisation, this is great if you want to Nordic walk long distances. You'll find information on paths, groups, events and challenges on their site. (See www.ldwa.org.uk)

Finally, of course, there are footpaths everywhere for you to explore. A point to consider is that if the path runs through high crops or very long grass, you may struggle to swing the poles effectively. Many a Nordic walker has ended up with poles aloft because the grass interrupts the swing of their poles (see Chapter 13 for advice).

JOINING OR SETTING UP A GROUP 8

JOINING A GROUP

The most popular way to enjoy Nordic walking is to join up with other people so that you can socialise and also enjoy the exercise and scenery together. The added benefit is that this usually means that an instructor or leader will have been involved in all of the planning so you do not have to worry too much about the route, timings, safety or other aspects of organisation.

In this chapter, you will find advice on what to look for when selecting a group. I will also discuss some successful models that have emerged in recent years.

There are a number of different Nordic walking groups across the world, each tending to attract those of similar ages, fitness levels and expectations. Some may be purely interested in technique or fitness, while others offer weight loss support, the opportunity to socialise and some guidance. Some are run as members' clubs, while others are run by charities or local authorities or operated as commercial enterprises. If you have already been taught correctly by a qualified instructor, you can find details of groups local to you, many of which are linked to or run by the instructors.

Figure 8.1 The Nordic Walking east London/Essex group

If you have not had any formal tuition, you may find that in order to join in regular Nordic walks you will need to demonstrate a good understanding of the technique (usually via a workshop) and provide other information in order to satisfy the instructor's insurance requirements. This may seem unnecessary to you, but all professional instructors will want to ensure that you can Nordic walk safely and are aware of the correct levels of intensity before taking responsibility for your well-being. They will also want to ensure that you are in the right group for your experience and other important criteria.

WHAT TO LOOK FOR IN A GROUP – WHAT DO YOU WANT?

When locating a suitable group, the first thing you need to do is ask yourself what you want to actually get out of your Nordic walking.

- Are you simply looking for a sociable Nordic walking experience?
- Or do you want to be continually motivated and pushed harder in order to get noticeable fitness results?

Most instructors offer a range of sessions for different fitness levels and abilities, and there are even some bespoke branded sessions to choose from. Generally, this will be made clear in the instructor's publicity materials. On the NWUK website, for instance, there are icons that make

Figure 8.2 Group performing hill drills on a workout walk

it clear what's on offer and you can book online. Below is a brief outline of what these types of sessions may entail.

Workout walks

These are generally shorter in duration, but tougher in intensity, their focus being on fitness improvement. The instructor should make it clear that there is an element of exercise planning as well as Nordic walking. This may include additional drills, circuits, strength training and speed work (outlined in Part 5).

If this type of Nordic walking session appeals to you make sure you check the following before booking:

- Is the instructor a qualified fitness professional with a clear understanding of anatomy, movement and exercise intensity (minimum REPs Level 2 – see page 178)?
- Does the instructor have a health screening system and will he/she ensure all class members have been taught basic technique?
- The class size should not exceed a ratio of 12 participants to one instructor, and unqualified leaders should never be left to supervise.
- Check that the instructor is fully insured to deliver fitness sessions outdoors.

Adventure walks

These are designed for the Nordic walker who has learned safe technique and wants to improve gradually through practice, while appreciating great places and good company. Many instructors and groups utilise fully trained walk leaders to lead those who have been taught how to make the most of their poles, and the focus is on having fun.

Good groups will have a clear schedule of walks and grade them according to ability,

Figure 8.3 Adventure walks are about exploring open spaces

Figure 8.4 Well-being walks are aimed at health improvement

making it easy to select those most suited to you.

If this type of session seems more like what you are seeking, make sure you check the following before booking:

- Are the leaders qualified, insured and trained in first aid?
- Does the instructor have a clear method of ensuring that no beginners attend regular walks without prior screening and tuition?
- Sessions are pre-booked

Well-being walks

For many regular Nordic walkers, health improvement is the main aim behind exercise and they are not quite ready to commit to a longer walk or too fast a pace. In this instance, a well-being session is the best option. These tend to be held in locations at which participants never feel that they are too far from the starting point and the pace is gentle. Many of these groups also specialise in the prevention or management of a number of health conditions and contain specific exercises designed to improve balance, strength, mobility and general fitness.

Many instructors and groups also offer well-being sessions specifically to encourage active ageing. This is generally promoted by age-related charities like Age UK or by physiotherapists working for fall prevention teams.

If this is what you are looking for make sure you check the following before booking:

- If you have a medical condition that would require specific consideration or have been advised by your doctor to exercise – make sure the instructor has the additional knowledge and skills to cater for it (many instructors are physiotherapists, for example).

- As above, check that sufficient health screening, systems and insurance are all in place.

Weight loss walks

Although regular Nordic walking will obviously be a great calorie burner, if weight loss is a major goal you may want find an instructor who can help you with healthy eating as well. Weight loss walks are generally specific classes that combine sensible eating advice (often in a workshop format) with walks that contain some intervals and strength work. Exercising for weight loss is quite complex and a good instructor will make sure the class has a mix of all the fitness elements required to help you manage your weight for good.

Things to check before you book:

- Has the instructor got the necessary skills and training to advise on weight loss?
- As above, check that sufficient health screening, systems and insurances are in place.

Nordic walking instructors are an innovative bunch and constantly come up with variety in terms of sessions. I have attended foraging walks, wildlife walks and a midsummer night vigil walk, to name but a few. One instructor in Wales is a master storyteller who weaves tales of myth and ancient legends for groups as they explore the stunning coastline. Thus, you are unlikely to get bored when Nordic walking, and all you have to do is check out local instructors on the NWUK websites and book an appropriate session.

To whet your appetite, I have outlined some case studies of various groups around the UK and hopefully these will prove that there is something for everyone on offer out there.

Case study: Nutters in the forest

When it comes to well-being and active ageing, Kim Prince and her group of Nordic walkers in the New Forest are the prime example of what can be achieved.

Kim became an instructor in 2009, while she was working as a sports injury therapist at Southampton Solent University. A qualified personal trainer, with additional specialisms in cardiac rehab, diabetes and obesity management, she began offering Nordic walking as part of a workplace heath programme. Interest grew among the local Age UK healthy walks programme and Kim began to teach regular tuition sessions for the 50+ age group. She soon realised that those she taught were desperate for safe regular Nordic walks and that many had medical conditions that meant they required a little more supervision and support.

She set up the Nordic Nutters Club in 2010 and has not looked back since. The club comprises more than 70 regular Nordic walkers, who attend between one and three walks a week and pay a quarterly fee. Kim is always

Figure 8.5 The 'Nordic Nutters', a group of Nordic walkers based in the New Forest

Figure 8.6 Age and ill health are not a barrier to the Nordic Nutters, who enjoy every step.

present because she understands each and every walker's specific needs, but she also has a number of volunteer leaders to help her manage the groups of up to 30 people per walk.

They often meet at a hotel car park in the forest, where they are a regular feature, chatting and encouraging each other. Kim is a skilled instructor who knows the right level for each walker, and she lets them fall into their natural pace, ensuring the least mobile are never left too far behind. All the walks are named after members of the group because this is the easiest way for them to remember the routes.

Testimonials from Nordic Nutters

'I have recently had one of my knees replaced and am waiting for the other to be done. I know I need to keep active in order to reduce weight to help me to cope with surgery and recovery. Nordic walking has been a lifeline and I would recommend it to anyone waiting for or recovering from joint replacements.' – *Jan*

'Nordic walking is life changing: my bone density had improved at the last scan; my doctors were delighted with me for taking part.' – *Pauline*

The group contains a lot of men, including Norman, who, at 86, is the oldest member. Perhaps the most surprising is John, who, as his wife explained, loathed exercise throughout a working life that involved commuting and being sedentary all day. He was apparently reluctant to attend the group at first, but now has withdrawal symptoms if he can't attend for any reason. John is always at the front of the group and does extra loops because he is so much faster – he also opens all the gates and waits for the whole group to pass through, which means he has to put on a spurt in order to get to the front again.

What makes the group work so well? The answer is simple: Kim. None of the group felt that they would simply go Nordic walking on their own, and all appreciate the fact that Kim ensures they have newsletters, trips and a variety of walks, as well as understanding their limitations and helping them to improve. None of them uses a gym, as one lady explains: 'Gyms and typical exercise classes are "isolating" where everyone is concentrating on the exercise or following an instructor. With Nordic walking, we can simply set off and chat.'

When I asked this group why they didn't just walk or ramble, rather than Nordic walk, they all agreed that it was the added boost and the support provided by the poles that made all the difference.

Case study: Ladies who promenade

Another instructor, Rosie Marler, has a more active clientele, who do not require the specific skills and guidance provided by Kim in Nordic Nutters. Mainly female, Rosie's clients attend because they enjoy meeting up and being active together, but, interestingly, Rosie does not offer any fitness or workout elements.

'It's all about the Nordic walking, socialising and the routes we select' says Rosie.

The group, called Promenading, meet up at a gallery in a stunning coastal town, where they enjoy a coffee and often have added guest speakers or demonstrations. It is this aspect of the group that seems to keep them all coming back regularly. This indicates that social interaction and being active are the driving forces behind Nordic walking's success, rather than specific health or fitness goals. They have regular adventure walks, during which they may go exploring over longer distances.

Once again, it is the skill of the instructor that is the key to developing a model that works. Rosie has developed a well-being group that enjoys relaxed social activity, rather than a 'workout'. Yet, Rosie's attention to detail, professional manner and planning ensure a lively schedule, and encourage people to stay with the group, rather than Nordic walk alone.

Figure 8.7 Rosie's Promenading group walk together for social interaction and fun

Case study: No-nonsense workouts

Two groups offering a range of levels – from well-being to tough circuits – are Exercise London, based on Hampstead Heath in London, and Beacon Outdoor Fitness, based in Dudley in the West Midlands. These groups have a high level of take-up from motivated individuals who are not necessarily looking to simply socialise or enjoy Nordic walking in beautiful locations. They want to work hard, get results and view the sessions as their regular exercise class. Even those attending the well-being sessions are looking to get measurable health or fitness improvements and want the interaction of professional instructors.

Exercise London is operated by leading Nordic walking expert Martin Christie, who has played an integral part in the development of the activity in the UK. His core classes take place in a leafy area to the north of central London which is very hilly (although his well-being group meet in Regents Park). Martin and his four instructors run classes of up to 15 participants (average class size is 8), led by a fitness-qualified instructor. These groups are motivated to work as hard as possible.

The classes comprise hill work, posture and technique drills, intervals and resistance work using bands, partners and body weight. Pace is always quite brisk and the focus is on fitness throughout. Clients can choose from over 10 sessions each week and must pre-book. Many pay in advance via booking cards or membership fees.

Figure 8.8 Group performing Ultimate Nordic circuit drills on a workout walk

Michael Horton, the owner of Beacon Outdoor fitness, runs workout-based classes in Dudley. His clientele are men and women, aged for the most part from their mid-50s to 75, although he does have one regular who is 85. The groups are 70 per cent female and like to feel they are exercising rather than simply adventure walking. They attend workout walks with approximately 10 people per session, during which they also use resistance bands, drills, hillwork and fast-paced Nordic walking based on the NWUK trek-fit programme.

COMMUNITY PROJECT GROUPS

There are fantastic projects that offer low-cost Nordic walking all over the UK. Charities such as Age UK coordinate schemes for senior walkers, while many local councils also offer programmes to encourage communities to be more active.

In many areas there are county 'sports partnerships', which plan, promote and coordinate Nordic walking sessions for all levels. Some have been funded to provide free sessions, while others charge nominal amounts in order to ensure sustainability.

Other organisations such as the Forestry Commission, the National Trust and English Heritage also support Nordic walking (see page 53 for more details) and many country parks host fantastic walk programmes led either by rangers or local instructors.

Expert tip

To find out if anything is on offer in your area you can visit your local council website or search by postcode on www.nordicwalking.co.uk

HEALTH CLUBS AND LEISURE CENTRES

A number of leisure centres across the UK now offer Nordic walking as part of their physical activity provision as they recognise that not everybody wants to exercise indoors. They are ideally placed to set up such schemes as they have highly trained and motivated staff who are used to dealing with those who are not accustomed to regular exercise and need extra support. This approach also works well for health clubs who understand that not everybody wants to exercise indoors, so don't be afraid to call up your local club or centre and ask if they offer Nordic walking. After all, if they know there is a demand it for it, they are more likely to add it to their schedule. A number of country clubs and spas do offer Nordic walking breaks too, often combined with revitalising treatments.

HEALTH-ORIENTATED GROUPS

Other unique groups have grown out of the need for individuals with health concerns to have the support of their expert advisers and peers. A great example of this is the Ladybird unit at Poole Hospital, Dorset, which runs regular sessions for women recovering from breast cancer. Many of the leaders have been though the programme themselves, and can help and support those just starting out on their journey of rehabilitation. Similar programmes for sufferers of Parkinson's disease and MS, and patients on stroke rehabilitation can also be found.

A team of physiotherapists from St George's NHS Health Trust in London offers classes as part of a fall prevention programme. Rather than waiting for frail people to fall and break bones they are being proactive, using a range of exercise solutions of which Nordic walking is ideal. (See pages 160–161 for more information.)

HOW TO SET UP A GROUP

Most of the groups across the UK started initially because the participants themselves wanted to find others to Nordic walk with. While it's tempting to think that you can simply meet up with others for a Nordic walk now and then, in reality it is important to remember that any group will require an element of communication and organisation if it is to grow and be able to cater for a mix of levels.

The most successful groups all have the same things in common:

- They have a fully qualified and inspirational instructor available to teach the basic Nordic walking technique and evaluate the abilities of all newcomers. Sometimes they will head up the group, but sometimes they are called in only when a beginner's course is required.
- Trained leaders are empowered to plan routes, risk-assess them and ensure all participants are kept safe.
- Routes and sessions are varied and well planned.
- Participants are supported and motivated and, if they want to progress, they are given the opportunity to do so.
- Beginners are always made to feel welcome and never feel that they are holding others back.

The NWUK delivery partner scheme helps new groups to both promote themselves and to keep growing because it provides support, marketing materials, leader training and even a range of programmes like weight loss and ski fit. If you would like to get a group going in your area, the first thing to consider is whether you would like to be the instructor, or would prefer to team up with a suitably qualified instructor in your area.

If the answer is 'yes' to becoming the instructor, see the following section, but if you would rather link up with a local professional, he/she can be found by searching the internet or through their own local marketing. Make sure you check that they are suitably qualified and insured to deliver what you require (especially if you have any medical concerns).

INSTRUCTOR TRAINING

People from any background can become Nordic walking instructors, as it is personality rather than prowess at technique or fitness that usually determines success. However, it is essential that they have an understanding of how the body works and how it can be improved massively with a structured activity programme, as well as an understanding of Nordic walking. Hopefully, our case studies and examples have made it clear that an effective instructor is far more than somebody who can simply pass on Nordic walking technique.

At NWUK, we feel it is essential that our instructors are as equally well trained as all other fitness professionals working in the sector and to that end, we have developed a level of training that provides our instructors with a formal, vocational Level 2 Fitness Instructor qualification.

The training is formulated in a manner that makes it as easy as possible to complete via online learning and a supportive practical session that covers technique, fault correction, route planning, health and safety, and class/business structure.

ONGOING SUPPORT

While some instructors have established businesses or jobs into which they can slot their Nordic walking (physiotherapists, personal trainers, etc.), many others are just starting out following a career change or retirement. They do not have the benefit of a current client base, websites or business systems, and will find it more difficult to get going and juggle the administration of managing a group with the demands of teaching people with varying needs. NWUK has developed a support network that provides the instructor with extra tuition, pre-written programmes, marketing materials, websites and opportunities to deliver on national contracts managed by the central team.

This approach helps keen new instructors to get started quickly and concentrate on their teaching rather than other aspects of developing a successful programme, which can be a bit daunting. These instructors can also issue Freedom Cards (see page 50) to their clients, thereby providing them with a host of benefits and the opportunity to attend walks and events with other participating instructors. Working together helps the instructors to provide a truly motivating range of sessions for all levels.

PART **FOUR**

4

NEED TO KNOW

EQUIPMENT FOR NORDIC WALKING

// **9**

Nordic walking poles consist of three main components:

1. Straps and handles.
2. Shaft.
3. Tips, paws and baskets.

They come in five major forms:

1. Fixed length.
2. Extendable.
3. Adjustable.
4. Telescopic.
5. Sprung poles.

This chapter covers all the components in turn, exploring the reasoning behind them and the different designs available according to manufacturer. It gives an objective view of the pros and cons of each type and helps you find the right ones for you.

We explore the five pole types and provide an overview of which type may be most suitable depending on how you intend to use them in the future. We will aim to dispel the myths that advocate various pole types based on claims made by some manufacturers.

THE THREE WALKING POLE COMPONENTS

The straps

These are by far the most important part of a Nordic walking pole because they determine whether it actually is one in the first place. Nordic walking poles always have a passive strap that allows the user to articulate the pole without over-gripping (see pages 149–150 for a detailed explanation of the process). The one exception to this is the Exerstrider strapless pole and that is covered in more detail in Chapter 2 (see pages 26–28).

To enable the user to achieve the necessary movement, it is essential that the straps are fixed to the pole while it is in use. Most manufacturers will provide different sizes, but Leki (a German manufacturer) has cleverly reversed the velcro closure so the standard strap fits both small and large hands. They also offer an option for medium to extra-large hands.

There are three types of attachment methods.

1. **Integral:** In this case, the strap is always attached to the pole, making it necessary for the user to remove the strap in order to avoid the pole getting in the way when opening gates

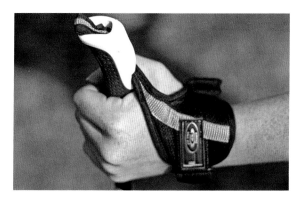

Figure 9.1 The integral strap, which does not disconnect from the pole

or taking off a layer of clothing. These straps often adjust via the loop at the top.

2. **Quick release straps:** These straps can be separated from the pole and also can be clicked back into place, using a plastic clip system. They vary slightly according to each manufacturer, but usually the user simply clicks the button at the top of the pole to remove them (see Figure 9.2).

3. **Shark:** Unique to the manufacturer Leki, the Shark is the simplest and most comfortable strap-fixing system. It only requires the strap to have a small loop between the thumb and forefinger (see Figure 9.3). It means that the strap is very comfortable, and easy to attach to and remove from the poles.

Note: Poles that simply have a looped strap like that pictured in Figure 9.4 are not designed for Nordic walking: the strap is designed to be looped around the wrist when trekking rather than performing an integral part of the action. Trekking straps are used as a way of keeping hold of the poles when it is necessary to ungrip, rather than as an essential part of the action. They can, however, also help to take pressure off the wrist by providing support – if used correctly. You will also note from Figure 9.5 that trekking pole handles tend to be more ergonomic because they are designed to be gripped; Nordic walking handles are not.

Figure 9.2 Removing the straps from the pole with a clip system

Figure 9.3 Leki Shark strap

Figure 9.4 A trekking pole with a looped strap

Figure 9.5 The ergonomic handle on a trekking pole

Handles

These vary a great deal. Cork has traditionally been used to provide a comfortable non-slip surface that feels warm in colder temperatures, but will also absorb sweat in warmer climates. There are more hard-wearing rubber and composite materials that can be utilised in designs with small recesses that help to avoid hand slippage when sweaty or wet. Cork is extremely comfortable and very popular; nonetheless, care must be taken when wearing rings as they may damage it. To avoid this, it is a good idea to either wear gloves or to remove any rings or jewellery. Most Nordic walking pole handles are a fairly simple shape, but some manufacturers have opted for more ergonomic grips on their poles, like those used on trekking poles. To reiterate, I do not find this kind of grip necessary as the hand contact with the handle is fairly minimal in Nordic walking, once you have mastered good technique.

Note: Exerstrider poles have a unique design of ergonomic handle that negates the use of a strap, but this does alter technique (see Chapter 2).

Figure 9.6 A Nordic walking pole with a cork handle and one with a rubbery grip to the handle

Pole shafts

The pole shaft is the main section of the pole, usually made of one of the following:
1. Aluminium/alloy.
2. Carbon.
3. Composite.

A good Nordic walking pole will have a tapered design, and be lightweight and strong. If the poles are adjustable, they will have adjustment points along the shafts and will be made up of two or three sections (i.e. telescopic; see types listed below).

The way in which different poles swing through the air can vary greatly, and this is due largely to the weight and composition of the pole.

Vibration is often cited as a negative aspect of poles. In fact, there are 'good' and 'bad' kinds of vibration. Poles are supposed to vibrate. The vibrations absorb the impact when planting the poles, especially on hard surfaces. The amount of vibration will vary according to the material from which the pole is made. A pole from a quality manufacturer will ensure that the vibration is equally balanced in the middle of the pole and does not transmit through to the hand. Bad vibration usually appears in the form of rattling from poor fittings or from vibration being transmitted through to the hand due to poor design or construction.

Poles are usually made from an aluminium alloy (a mixture of metals in which aluminium is the predominant metal) that has a high strength-to-weight ratio. Aluminium, as a material, proves light and strong, and has the advantage that if the poles are slightly damaged or bent, you may be able to bend them back (within reason).

The mixture of materials used can vary greatly from one manufacturer to another. Composite materials vary with a mixture of different components such as fibreglass, resins, plastics and sometimes carbon woven in.

Carbon is stiff, light, very strong and provides a much more precise action than most comparable materials. The greater the carbon content, the less vibration. As a result, a carbon pole can be less forgiving, an aspect that should be taken into consideration if you have contra-indications, such as arthritis or a wrist injury.

If you encounter a strong cross-wind while walking, the lightness of the carbon poles can also sometimes be an issue. Carbon content can vary between 10 and 100 per cent: even a pole with a 20 per cent carbon content will feel quite different to one with none. Although carbon poles have a very strong construction overall, they are not indestructible. You need to look after them, as they can be easily scratched or scuffed. It is worth investing in a bag to protect them when travelling or when they are in storage.

Pole tips, 'paws' and baskets

Most Nordic walking poles have tungsten tips on the bottom that are covered by a removable rubber 'paw'. The tips are ideal for use on softer ground as they will 'bite' and allow you a good clean plant of the pole. On some poles, you will find a sharp angular metal 'speed tip'. These are normally fitted to performance-type poles, providing better grip when applying more pressure on the pole plant. **Be warned:** these tips are very sharp and can cut through the top of a lightweight shoe should you plant the pole awkwardly.

The rubber paws are for use on hard surfaces and should *always* be an angled design. The pole is at an angle when it strikes the ground and this shape allows the base of the paw to be flat against the ground, which is necessary to provide enough grip for you to be able to gain propulsion. A straight rubber paw, like the ones found on trekking poles, will slip when Nordic walking. Straight rubber paws are designed for the poles to be upright.

Figure 9.7 The tungsten tip found on most Nordic walking poles (left) and the speed tip found on some 'performance' poles

Figure 9.8 An angled rubber paw (left) compared with a pole with a trekking paw

Figure 9.9 Silent spike paw

Figure 9.10 The smart tip paw can be slipped back and forwards in order to expose or cover the tungsten tip

The silent spike paws, made by Leki, comprise a rubber paw that includes tungsten tips. This invention has improved the surface grip on tarmac, for example, but also has proved suitable for most other surfaces. That means there is no need to remove or replace paws mid-walk. When walking on hard surfaces, these tips are silent, hence the name – unlike the typical metal tip that makes an annoying tapping sound. In the end, however, whichever paw you choose is a question of personal choice, and people either swear by silent spike paws or don't get on with them at all.

Another recent innovation is the smart tip paw which does not need to be removed completely but can be flicked down to cover the tip and back to expose again it as required. Although this minimises the risk of losing paws, it does require regular cleaning in order to function properly and you are likely to get muddy hands when changing it, an unpopular aspect of any paw changing.

Exerstrider poles have an extremely well-designed highly flexible paw, and they also supply the bell paw, a larger, non-angled paw, ideal

Figure 9.11 Exerstrider paws are very flexible and supply superior stability

Figure 9.12 Snow baskets stop poles sinking too deep in soft snow or sand

for helping stability. They are popular with the wellness, care-home and seniors' markets.

Baskets are designed to stop the pole embedding itself too deep into soft ground. You can purchase different size baskets according to the terrain. For example, if you regularly walk in sand or snow, you may want to consider fitting a wider basket.

POLE TYPES

Fixed length

The pole is made up of one single shaft with no size adjustments. Most manufacturers supply fixed-length poles in 5cm increments from 100cm up to 130cm.

Extendable

The pole is made up primarily of one long shaft but has an extension below the handle that allows the user to adjust the pole to the desired length. Vibration is minimised because the adjustment is not in the centre of the shaft. Some manufacturers (such as Leki) provide 10cm of extension (and ideally you need to be somewhere in the middle when choosing correct length), while others, such as Gabel (see Figure 9.15), have models that will extend out to 30cm.

Figure 9.14 Quick-release lock on a Leki Flash Vario pole

Figure 9.15 Right: The Gabel Inverso Alu – an extendable pole

Figure 9.13 The main types of Nordic walking pole, from left to right: fixed, extendable, adjustable, telescopic, Exerstrider and trekking

The mechanism of adjustment can either be the typical twisting action with an expanding part inside the lower shaft or a quick lock–lever mechanism. Although the quick-release lever may add some 30g to the pole's weight, because it sits just below the handle, it does not affect the swing of the pole.

Adjustable

The pole is made up of two pieces of metal, with an adjustment mechanism in the *centre* of the shaft. This enables the user to adjust the pole to exactly the required length by loosening the adjuster and sliding the two pieces up or down and then re tightening it again. Most poles will adjust from 100 to 130cm. The vast majority of poles sold in the UK are fully adjustable and they are completely suitable for all levels of Nordic walking. Note, however, that these poles are still fairly long when broken down.

Figure 9.16 Leki Prestige – a fully adjustable pole

Figure 9.17 Leki Traveller – a three-part telescopic pole

Telescopic

As the name suggests, these poles come in three sections that can be loosened either to slide into each other (like a telescopic umbrella), making them easy to fold away, or that can be extended out to the required length and tightened in the same way as with the adjustable poles discussed above. The main benefit of these poles is that they can be carried easily, especially on public transport and on planes.

Sprung poles

Sprung poles are not appropriate for Nordic walking, but they are worth mentioning because you may come across them. Many trekking poles have shock absorption built into them and they have become very popular with ramblers as they reduce impact when planted. There are also a few sprung poles being marketed that are masquerading as Nordic walking poles, with a trekking handle and strap. Our expert team tested them extensively and found that while they can provide an arm work-out, they contradict the whole principle of Nordic walking by absorbing all the energy that would typically propel you forwards.

WHAT KIND OF POLES SHOULD YOU CHOOSE? OUR RECOMMENDATIONS

Until recently, it has largely been accepted that users should only select fixed-length carbon poles because other types were deemed unsafe, heavy and/or caused too much vibration. We don't believe this and think that in many cases these ideas may have arisen through targeted marketing by manufacturers supporting non-adjustable poles. Quality adjustable or extendable poles can be a suitable choice for a range of Nordic walkers – from beginners to more advanced participants. They have their merits, but they have limitations as well. The following section will hopefully help you make an informed choice when choosing a Nordic walking pole, by outlining what we feel are the pros and cons of each type.

Fixed-length poles are simple, uncomplicated pieces of equipment that are usually cheaper than other kinds of poles. They also minimise the opportunity of any unwanted vibration. This is all great if you happen to require the exact lengths available. Unfortunately, they only come in 5cm increments, which means that many people are walking using the wrong length pole – even 1 or 2cm in length can make all the difference to pole gripping when planted, especially on hard surfaces. Many experts believe that having the wrong length pole can cause more discomfort in the long term than the tiny increase (if any) in bad vibration or weight more likely with a pole that is adjustable.

That said, if necessary, you can always shorten a fixed-length pole by removing the handle (usually glued on), cutting a section from the top of the shaft and refixing the handle back on. This does provide a made-to-measure option, but you can't extend it back again if you then find it too short.

These days the **adjustment systems** on good makes of poles like Leki, Gabel and Exerstrider are very efficient. They are lightweight, ensure minimal vibration and are exceedingly strong. In fact, they will bear up to 130–140kg of downward pressure with no problem at all. If you are using them for Nordic walking, as intended, they will last for years and are completely safe.

Note: you do need to ensure you occasionally clean the parts and clear away any mud, sand or grit.

---

1 Have you mastered the Nordic walking technique?

Yes	No
Advice Select any type as long as you are confident in the size required; if not stick with adjustable or extendable.	**Advice** Select adjustable poles at this stage – composite will depend on question 2 below.

---

2 Do you plan to use your poles more than twice a week?

Yes	No
Advice Opt for extendable poles or higher carbon content if you can afford to.	**Advice** Any composite and pole type should be fine.

---

3 Will you be regularly travelling abroad or on public transport with your poles?

Yes	No
Advice Invest in good-quality telescopic poles or have a second pair for travelling.	**Advice** Avoid telescopic poles for regular Nordic walking unless you are prepared to pay for carbon versions.

---

4 What is your budget?

Modest	Reasonable	Unlimited
Opt for a good make that fits all of your other criteria above and is sold by a reputable retailer who understands Nordic walking. Note: Fixed-length poles are cheaper, but getting the wrong size will cost more in the long run.	Opt for the most popular brands, seek out advanced features like 'shark straps' and specialised paws, and go for a higher carbon content where possible.	Opt for 100 per cent carbon and design features that improve comfort and ease of use. If you are new to Nordic walking opt for an extendable pole in case your technique improves to a level that will require you to lengthen the poles.

Figure 9.17 Questions to ask yourself when choosing Nordic poles

Expert tip

If you have yet to learn the Nordic walking technique, it is inadvisable for you to select a one-piece pole at the outset. This is because it's very common for people to change posture and fitness in the early days of training, and you may find the one-piece poles are too small when you want to progress your technique in the future. Similarly, if the poles are too long or too short they will impede your ability to gain good Nordic walking technique in the long term.

Figure 9.18 An instructor assesses the pole height for a client

Other factors to to help you make your Nordic walking pole selection:

- **The weight of the pole** – the lighter the better, if you are looking for top performance.
- **The make** – try to avoid cheaper brands. It's important to go for the established makes like Leki, Gabel, Swix and Kompardell – these companies actually manufacture ski poles too, and have invested greatly in the development of their products. Less well-known brands to the Nordic walking market may be copies made in the Far East, and the quality and longevity may be difficult to assess.
- **Strap adjustment and comfort** – see earlier in this chapter for the various types (pages 66–67).
- **Handle materials** – do you prefer cork or a rubber-style grip? (See page 68.)
- **Tips/paws** – are you happy to remove rubber paws when you want to move from hard surfaces onto grass or would you rather flip a smart tip?

GETTING THE POLE HEIGHT CORRECT

As previously discussed in this chapter, a couple of centimetres adjustment to your pole length can make a huge amount of difference to your technique and how much propulsion you gain each time you plant the pole. NWUK believes that it is always best to start people off using adjustable poles and to check them every four weeks in the early stages.

Here's how to get the best basic pole size:
Stand up straight with your elbow fixed down the side of the body and the pole held vertically with the elbow at approximately a 90 degree angle (see Figure 9.18). The wrist should be slightly lower than the elbow at a gradient that would allow water to trickle down the arm.

If you are not sure you have got it right, see common faults in Chapter 16. Many arise from an incorrect pole height.

Expert tip

No two people are exactly the same, and joint mobility, limb proportion, walking speed and individual Nordic walking goals will influence the right pole length for any particular person. It is always a good idea to get a qualified instructor to set you up in the first instance and keep an eye on your progress. Initially, it is all about comfort, and instinctively feeling that the technique is flowing and, above all, is actually providing propulsion.

Figure 9.20 The paw should engage fully with the ground when the pole is planted

GETTING SET UP TO GO

Once you have selected your poles, make sure they are set up correctly before you start Nordic walking.

Always perform these **quick checks**:

- Have you pre-sized the poles?
- Once you've made any adjustment have you made sure everything has been tightened and locked tight? You don't want the poles to collapse once pressure is applied.

Figure 9.19 Straps are usually labelled 'L' and 'R' to ensure you get them right

- Are the straps on the correct hands? They will usually be marked with 'L' and 'R'.
- Are they on tight enough? Loose straps will affect your ability to put power through them effectively and can cause discomfort.
- Are the paws on your poles facing the right way and on tight?

TROUBLE SHOOTING AND MAINTENANCE

Most poles are pretty simple to operate and adjust, but just in case you are experiencing any difficulties, here is some advice on how to keep your poles in good working order.

Twizzling: The NWUK retail team use this term for when an adjustable pole fails to tighten at the chosen length. This occurs when the pole has been excessively turned in order to unlock. Although it is very simple to sort out, if it's not addressed, it can cause major frustration just before a walk. It often occurs on poles used in teaching packs because of the volume of use and the need to continually adjust them. Most home purchasers are less likely to keep adjusting the pole once they have found their desired height.

Figure 9.21 shows how the locking mechanism works and will enable you to readjust the poles and get on your way.

There are three basic steps:

1. Take the poles apart completely so you have the bottom section in one hand and the upper section in the other.
2. You will see that the super-lock mechanism on Leki poles contains an expander (shown in blue in the diagram) – give this a half turn to the left.
3. Put the pole ends back together and they should now lock again.

Figure 9.21 The locking mechanism inside Leki poles

Keypoints

Tips for looking after your poles to ensure they last for several years:

- Remove paws after a muddy walk or they will stick on tight.
- Clean poles with a damp cloth periodically and rinse straps in lukewarm water.
- Loosen height adjustment periodically and retighten or the pole may get fused.
- If storing the poles it is best to reduce them down rather than leave tightened, and store them in a warm, dry place.
- Transport poles in a padded pole bag or hard-pole case to avoid knocks to the side or damage from heavy items being placed on top of them.

WHAT TO WEAR WHEN NORDIC WALKING

10

FOOTWEAR

Nordic walking requires flexible-soled walking shoes or trainers that are ideally waterproof. Many people assume that heavy, leather walking boots will be required, but these can actually make it difficult to achieve a good Nordic walking technique because they are generally heavier and less flexible than the latest walking shoe styles. Similarly, running shoes are also not usually designed to suit the Nordic walking gait, which requires the foot to be in contact with the ground for far longer, a much more centred heel strike and a much more pronounced push from the toe than used in running.

When choosing a shoe, the first thing to consider is **comfort**. Different makes of shoes tend to suit those with different types of gait or foot type (wide, narrow, high arch, etc.) and most people quickly find a brand that generally suits them.

The key features to look out for are:
- Flexibility in the forefoot in order to allow you to push off from the toes.
- Adequate heel cushioning as good Nordic walking technique involves a heel strike.
- The shoe should not slip at the heel or rub when the foot rolls through the stride.

- Avoid footwear that is too high around the ankle as this can cause rubbing at the front when the toe is raised for the heel strike.
- A snug fit to avoid the foot slipping forwards which can cause the toes to hit the toe box and become bruised.
- A relatively lightweight shoe.
- Ideally select a waterproof shoe. There is nothing worse than wet feet on a long walk. Goretex or similar fabrics are both breathable and waterproof, so try to select these if possible or you will end up with dry, but 'sweaty' feet.

Shoes with most of these key features will usually be found at specialist outdoor stores and could be in the walking, trekking or trial running sections. Sometimes they are labelled as 'XC' (cross-country), multi-terrain or trail shoes.

Styles vary dramatically, from lightweight styles aimed at the fast competitive trail racer to heavier more robust styles for the distance walker. The latter will generally provide more ankle support. This is advisable if you are likely to be covering rough ground, although I would not personally advise shoes or boots that cover the ankle.

When trying shoes on, remember to wear the type of socks you intend to use when Nordic walking (see page 81 for advice) and try to ensure your feet are not too cold. It is a good idea to try shoes on in the afternoon because feet tend to swell throughout the day.

Make sure that your toes are not right at the end of the toe box and, where possible, seek advice from an assistant who has been trained to ensure a good fit. The general guide is to allow a thumb's width between the end of the toe and the end of the shoe, but this is difficult to work out if the shoe has a sturdy toe box that doesn't allow you to feel where the toes actually is. I usually find that specialist outdoor stores and running shops are better than discount stores or general shoe retailers, and some are experts on gait analysis and can advise on specialist insoles.

If you have problems with shoes collapsing to one side, wearing unevenly or causing foot pain, it is a good idea to have your gait analysed. Most of the above issues can be corrected by selecting the correct shoe or using a specialist insole. Podiatrists and foot health practitioners are now widely available, but a physiotherapist can also provide advice on your gait style and any potential problems it may cause. Remember, if you are looking to improve your health and well-being by being more active, it is important to get things right from the start. There is no point starting out in ill-fitting or unsuitable shoes as this could lead to a range of injuries that are likely to quash your effects in the longer term.

Buying online is not advisable unless the retailer offers a sizing service or you are sure that you know the sizing and style of the make you are selecting. Most Nordic walkers have a favourite brand and keep an eye out for bargains as the styles change each season.

Figure 10.1 Merrell and Aku, two of the makes NWUK recommends

When NWUK asked instructors and their clients to list their favourite shoes, the following brands were most popular: Merrell, North Face, Salomon, Aku and Asics.

Fitness walking shoes

In recent years, walking has become recognised as an effective way to exercise and this has led to a range of shoes targeted at those walking for fitness. While some manufacturers claim that you can become 'toned' simply by wearing their shoes, others do contain technology and innovations designed to provide benefits to the wearer.

BAREFOOT WALKING SHOES

Barefoot walking and running are enjoying an explosion in popularity at the moment, and the concept is simple. Humans were originally designed to walk without shoes, and our feet contain a host of tiny bones and muscles that work together to help us move, stand and balance. Many people believe that over the years, shoes have altered the way we walk, potentially leading to injuries and ill health. Research has shown that children walk differently barefoot, compared with when wearing shoes, and in countries in which a high proportion of people have no footwear, they tend to suffer far fewer injuries than those wearing shoes.

Walking and running barefoot is not practical for most of us, and so a range of shoes that help us to achieve this more natural gait have appeared. There is not enough evidence yet to prove that they improve injury levels and balance. Their popularity, however, suggests that they are extremely comfortable. These types of shoes should always be introduced gradually, especially for exercise walking or running.

Most brands make barefoot shoes, but one of the pioneers is Vivobarefoot (www.vivobarefoot.com).

MASAI BAREFOOOT TECHNOLOGY SHOES

Developed in the 1990s, these were one of the first fitness walking shoes based on the 'rocker sole' concept and should not be confused with the trend for barefoot walking/running outlined in the section above. The concept was born from watching how Masai warriors walked barefoot on soft and uneven ground. The basic principle of these shoes is that the constant instability causes the activation of a number of small muscles as the body continually works to stabilise itself.

MBTs, as they are known, create the instability via a cut-away heel that makes the walker balance on the middle part of the sole. This makes them totally unsuitable for Nordic walking, which requires a solid heel strike, a conscious roll through the mid-foot and a push-off from the toe. Both MBTs and Nordic walking have a place to play in toning the lower body and working on posture, but used together they cancel out each other's benefits.

SPRINGBOOST SHOES

This Swiss walking shoe manufacturer bases its manufacturing science on dorsi-flexion technology, a method of placing the heel lower than the ball of the foot via interchangeable insoles. Founded at the renowned Federal Institute of Technology in Lausanne, it has a dedicated customer base who believe in the postural and performance-enhancing benefits of this system, which promotes proper curvature of the spine. Each pair comes with two in-soles that enable the user gradually to get accustomed to dorsi-flexion before it is increased to really add intensity. Springboost makes specific waterproof and lightweight walking shoes, and their use in our Nordic walking trials has been very positive so far.

REEBOK 'EASYTONE' AND SKECHERS 'SHAPE UP' SHOES

These are also marketed as fitness walking shoes, with the former also using 'instability' as the toning element, although that is created by the movement of air through the sole.

Figure 10.2 The Springboost walking shoe has dorsiflexion technology

Skechers have a unique slip-on walking shoe for ladies (the 'GOwalk') that is exceptionally lightweight and easy to get on and off. Made in a mesh fabric, these shoes are designed to be worn without socks because they are breathable and contain a built-in, anti-microbial sock liner. They do not look like a 'fitness shoe' so are ideal for use with non-fitness clothing (great for those of us who Nordic walk to work.)

The GOwalk 2 is a more technical all-day, everyday comfortable shoe that is great for walking. The technology ('V-Stride') comprises a unique, angled heel that does seem to promote a good walking technique. The shoe's extreme flexibility allows a good roll through the foot and they also contain a special mid-sole that absorbs impact.

Note: For many of the above innovations, there is little research available to make an accurate assessment of their suitability in the long term. Some physical therapists are convinced that over-engineered shoes cause more injuries than no shoes at all, and that leads us back to the top of this section and the need to evaluate your gait and to think carefully about what you put on your feet. This is especially so if you have ever suffered from foot, knee, back or hip pain.

Finally, there is no point investing in expensive shoes if you then put on a pair of cheap socks with no technical features or special padding.

CLOTHING

As Nordic walking is suitable for all terrains, locations and weather conditions, and at any level from competitions to well-being, there is a vast array of clothing that could be deemed suitable. In most cases, what you wear is governed by the factors mentioned, and also personal choice.

The general rule of thumb is to select layers of clothing that can be added or removed if the weather and temperature changes. This process also means that you can stay warm without too much bulky clothing because air becomes trapped between the layers, providing insulation. Each layer has its own function and there are a few basic rules to help you get it right – starting from the bottom layer.

UNDERWEAR

While many people concentrate on the top layer, it is just as important to ensure that your underwear is comfortable. Repetitive movement and getting hot and sweaty can be a lethal combination, so make sure that your base layers are made of breathable materials and are *never* too tight.

These days there are ranges of highly technical underwear that actually help to regulate your

Figure 10.3 Skechers GOwalk lightweight shoe

Figure 10.4 Skechers GOwalk 2 lightweight shoe

body temperature and affect performance. The X-Bionic trekking underwear range, for instance, provides significantly increased comfort for those using backpacks because it has AirDuct pads on the shoulders and hips that help to spread the pressure of the pack over a wide proportion of the body. The special weave of the pads also provides ventilation and cooling for those sweatier parts of the body, including sweat traps under the arms. A final bonus is that the whole X-Bionic range utilises technology that prevents that awful chilling from damp, sweaty clothing when you stop after vigorous activity. The 3D pads actually provide insulation so that you feel comfortable both during the activity and when you stop. In fact, these garments reduce the need for a base layer (see below).

Sports bras

It is a common mistake to think that only runners need to wear sports bras. Nordic walking is quite a smooth action, but it will lead to movement of the breasts. It is important to ensure you have adequate support or this movement will stretch the connective tissue around the breasts (known as Cooper's ligaments). That will lead to sagging. As these ligaments are not actually muscles, no amount of training will restore them once damage has been done, so prevention is the answer.

Sports bras not only provide this vital support, but also have wide comfy straps that do not dig into the shoulders (especially good if you are using a rucksack), and good ones don't have clips or metal parts that may rub or cause irritation. Another important benefit is that they are generally breathable and easy to wash and dry, so you can stick them in with your other kit after each walk.

Figure 10.5 X-Bionic produce a range of underwear to help regulate body temperature and impact on performance

SOCKS

Trekkers and walkers traditionally choose thick socks (often made of wool) to prevent blisters when wearing leather boots, while runners tend to select lightweight, breathable socks with blister protection panels and technical features such as silver to aid with deodorising. Nordic walkers require both the protection of a thicker sock and also the cooling, lightweight element favoured by runners. To enjoy Nordic walking, it is essential that you choose socks that are supremely comfortable, allow your feet to breathe and have padding/protection in the right places. One range called X-Socks make specific Nordic walking socks, which, although expensive, provide a host of features that, once experienced, are difficult to live without.

The socks contain a unique anti-shuffling footbed that is thicker under the arch of the foot than it is at the heel and toes. This actually aids the rolling action of the foot, while special channels also help to wick sweat away from the foot to keep it cool and dry. Finally there is specific protection for the toes, Achilles tendon and even over the in-step as all of these areas are subject to wear and chaffing when Nordic walking. The socks are lightweight despite also containing a special X-shaped support for the ankles, rather like having a bandage on to protect against strains.

Figure 10.6 Nordic walking-specific X Socks

Waterproof socks

These are excellent if you prefer non-waterproof shoes and yet hate getting your wet feet. Waterproof shoes tend to be more expensive than non-waterproof shoes and although they are 'breathable', they are not as cool to wear as the more lightweight mesh upper shoes designed for summer walking. However, the latter can cause problems if you walk through wet grass or encounter a sudden rainstorm and that's where waterproof socks come in. There is nothing worse than water squishing between your toes with every step, and it can chill your feet too. So, wearing waterproof socks such as Sealskinz is a good idea if you prefer non-waterproof shoes. The science is in the fabric and composition of these socks, which are made up of three layers:

1. An inner layer of merino wool and other materials designed to worn next to the skin. This layer is warm, comfortable, high wicking and anti-microbial.
2. The membrane barrier is both waterproof and breathable. It's impervious to water but will allow sweat, in the form of water molecules, to pass through it. This keeps the feet dry and comfortable.
3. The outer layer provides the first layer of protection against the elements.

BASE LAYER

Any outdoor enthusiast will tell you that it is important to 'layer up', and it all starts with what you put next to your skin. The best fabrics to wear close to the skin are merino wool, bamboo or synthetic technical fibres like microfibre, CoolTech and polyesters that will wick away moisture rather than absorb it. The aim is to wick the moisture away into the next layer of clothing and then to allow it to evaporate. This is why it is important to always select breathable garments for each layer, if possible. This process will keep your skin area dry, and that in turn ensures you feel comfortable and do not chill. When searching for technical synthetic base layers, remember to check for anti-bacterial properties too or the garment will soon smell unbearable.

Base layers come as long or short-sleeved styles and are ideal for use in all weathers.

Figure 10.7 A base layer by X-Bionic

Figure 10.8 Examples of long- and short-sleeved mid-layers for different conditions

MID-LAYER

This is the layer that provides insulation. A range of garments – from fleeces to gilets – provide warmth, without being too bulky. This layer also needs to be breathable and can be made from merino wool or fleece fabrics, both of which are lightweight and can come in different grades of insulation. The more technical ones are made by brands such as Polartec or Thinsulate; the former has a graded range based on how much insulation you require. Other features may include windproofing and zips that can be used to vent the garments if needed.

Some of the gilets are made from goose down, which is incredibly lightweight and does squash down very small for packing. The downside is if it gets wet, you will know about it. Gilets provide a warm (and sometimes even windproof) layer for the body; it does not feel too bulky under a jacket and gives freedom of movement for the arms.

In the summer months, lightweight shirts feel cool and loose, and can be paired with a gilet, but in cooler temperatures, a more insulated long-sleeve mid-layer is a good idea.

TROUSERS

Nordic walkers tend to fall into two categories when it comes to legwear. While one group favour walking shorts and/or outdoor technical trousers, the other group prefers sleeker running-style leggings or tights. Both are ideal and comfortable; however, trousers should not be too wide as this can impede the poles. Try to select materials that are quick to dry or waterproof, and allow for ease of movement (some have flexible knee joints, for instance). Always avoid heavy non-waterproof fabrics like jeans because if these get wet they will cling, restrict movement and feel very uncomfortable.

Tights can come in a variety of thicknesses, and the insulated ones do actually feel warmer than most trousers I have tried. However, in summer I think that the breathable trousers and shorts are a better bet.

Figure 10.9 Trilith pants by XBionic

Figure 10.10 An outer shell jacket

SHELL OR TOP LAYER

This is the most important of all the layers because it is the one that keeps the wind and rain out, and ideally lets your body breathe. If you are following the layering principle, this outer jacket can literally be a 'shell' that is waterproof and windproof. This will also make it light and easy to pack away when not required. However, top layer jackets do come with additional levels of insulation.

You will also come across 'soft shell' items that are generally water resistant, windproof, lightweight and breathable. These are great for everyday wear but will not keep you totally dry in foul weather unless you invest in the latest highly technical ranges. Choose them for chilly days on which maybe only a shower is forecast. For really wet days, wear a hard shell, with layers beneath.

The key features to look out for in hard shell jackets are sealed zips (including on pockets), 100 per cent waterproof (not shower-proof) and breathability. You do also need the fit to be loose enough to allow you to add layers beneath it, when required.

The final outer shell that you should carry in inclement weather is a pair of fully waterproof over-trousers. These are designed to pop over your usual trousers and the best ones have an elasticated waistband and poppers or studs up the sides of the legs so you can get them on quickly if the heavens open. Another way to protect the lower legs when walking in longer grass or through bracken is to wear a pair of waterproof gaiters that clip under your shoes or boots and zip up at the sides. These also prevent water from entering the top of your footwear.

A pair of great-value over-trousers are the Regatta 'Packaway' over-trousers, which have all the features mentioned above, and are easy to scrunch up and pack into your backpack too.

Expert tip

Waterproof breathable fabrics like GoreTex come in a range of grades for different protection levels. Where possible, seek advice from outdoor store professionals who really understand the technology. As with most things, the price is generally a good guide to the level of protection that the fabric will provide.

HATS AND GLOVES

It's easy to think that these items are only important in the winter months, but a hat is a good idea in summer, while gloves are a must if using poles for any length of time.

Hats come in a variety of shapes and sizes, but I prefer lightweight caps or visors in summer as these have the added benefit of shading the face and protecting the eyes. Visors are ideal as they keep the head cool, but in really strong sun it is advisable to cover the whole head and you can get cool-tech fabrics or mesh caps that do the job.

You can find caps that include a neck panel too, which is a sensible way to avoid sunstroke.

In cold weather, I prefer a thermal fleece or softshell hat that covers the ears, and one of the most functional is the Sealskinz beanie, which is totally waterproof too.

Probably the most adaptable item I keep in my backpack is the Buff, a seamless tube of microfibre material that can be worn several ways on the head and around the neck. I find it invaluable as a way to keep the chill off the neck area and often wear it as a bandana or full hat too. A favourite of outdoor enthusiasts, these come in a variety of designs and scrunch up when not required. They also wick away moisture and help to keep you cool in hot weather, as well as warm when it's chilly. A final benefit is that they can be worn wound around the wrist and used as a sweatband in really hot weather as well.

Sunglasses

When dressing for the outdoors in any weather, do not forget to think about eye protection. UV rays can cause both short-term and long-term damage to the eyes so a pair of sunglasses should become part of your Nordic walking kit.

Most good brands will provide adequate UVB protection (ideally blocking up to 99 per cent of rays), but it is also a good idea to select a pair that block out UVA rays as well.

Figure 10.11 A waterproof beanie hat by Sealskinz

Lens tints can come in a variety of colours and, without getting too technical, it's a good idea to understand the basic differences. They are:

- Darker tints like browns, greys, blues and greens are great in bright sunlight as they reduce glare.
- Yellowy/amber/gold tints are better in poorer light as they filter out blue light, which helps to identify uneven ground.
- Polarised lenses are brilliant for reducing the glare from water, sandy desert-like terrain and so on, but they can sometimes be a tad too dark for shadowy conditions.

Some really good brands do come with interchangeable lenses, but I think it's best to just be aware of the differences and choose a good-quality pair that are comfortable.

Other factors to look for are:

- Lightweight cleanable frames.
- Frames that either hold the lens away from the face or have ventilation panels to stop them fogging up when you get sweaty.
- More 'sporty' or wrap-around styles that help with side glare and comfort when on the move.

WHAT TO CARRY WHEN NORDIC WALKING

11

What you carry will depend on a number of factors:

1. How long you will be out, and with whom.
2. The weather conditions.
3. The type of terrain and locality.
4. The type of session you will be undertaking (i.e. fitness, social, distance trek, race etc.).

Whatever you do decide to pack, there are a few golden rules when choosing the correct backpack or waist belt to carry them in.

BACKPACKS

The key features to look out for when choosing a backpack suitable for Nordic walking is that it is not too wide, as this will impede the natural swing of the arms. You also need to ensure that it is lightweight, and ideally has a waist strap and chest strap to prevent it bouncing as you stride and help spread the load evenly. These types of backpacks will generally be labelled as 'daypacks' or 'sports packs', and are often graded by the volume they will accommodate – about 15 litres or under is ideal. For a full day's walking, you may want to go up to about 22 litres as that will give you room for lunch, emergency supplies, water and additional clothing.

Other ideal features are:

- Padded shoulder straps.
- Waterproof exterior or pull over waterproof cover.
- Mesh pockets for energy drinks and water bottles that are easy to reach when the pack is on your back.
- Small accessible compartment for your keys and phone.
- An airflow system – this is a tensioned mesh back that creates an air space between the bag and your back. This is great for longer walks as it stops you getting hot and sweaty on your back, but it is less suitable for fitness walking.

WAIST BELTS

For fitness walking a waist belt may be preferable and these come in a range of sizes.

The smallest is a tiny neoprene pouch that simply contains phone, keys, money and so on, which is suitable for a short training walk, where you may not require water. I prefer to use a waist pouch rather than the armband types that are also available.

When teaching and for longer walks I would advise a larger pack that ensures adequate hydration

Figure 11.1 The SpeedLite 15-litre backpack is an ideal size for a short to medium-distance walk; for longer full-day walks, a larger pack may be advisable

Figure 11.2 The Deuter Pulse Four is suitable for use when teaching or for longer walks

and emergency essentials, and for this a **Deuter Pulse Four** (see Figure 11.2) is suitable. It has a water bottle holder, phone and key pockets and enough room for a first aid kit, energy bar and other essentials. It only has space for a very thin layer of clothing and personally if I think I might be in need of that or further supplies, I would opt for a backpack as anything with more weight would make the waist belt unsuitable. There are two smaller waist belts in the Deuter Pulse range that offer a smaller amount of general space, but are great for essentials.

HYDRATION SYSTEM

Many packs these days also allow you to use a hydration 'bladder' that you can fill with water. This can then be accessed via a tube that you can reach without removing the pack. The bladders can usually be purchased separately but it is important to select a pack that has the correct holes for the drinking tubes and a designated compartment for the bladder. While this is a more balanced way to transport liquids, it is important to keep every part of the system clean, including all tubing.

FIRST AID KIT

There are plenty of lightweight kits designed for use outdoors. Evaluate the things you would be most likely to use in relation to where you intend to walk and prepare your kit accordingly. A good kit will contain many of the items highlighted below, and they can be purchased separately and added to make your own personalised pack. None of the items take up too much space and so they can be taken on most outings without too much discomfort.

Tick removers

Don't walk without these, especially in areas with bracken or a significant deer population. Tick bites can lead to serious illnesses and although preventing bites is preferable, it is wise to check for and remove ticks immediately, using a specially designed tool rather than burning them with match heads or smothering them with petroleum jelly. Tick removers come in many forms, but the simplicity of the small hook-and-twist type like the O'Tom Tick Twister (www.otom.com) is particularly helpful.

Blister packs or foot oil

When a blister begins to form you need to act quickly, and there is no better way to prevent it from causing pain and getting worse than to cover with a specialised blister plaster. Unlike ordinary plasters, these provide padding, encourage healing and do not curl up or rub off. You can also get a blister prevention stick that reduces friction and rubbing (see www.compeed.co.uk) or foot oil that conditions the feet (see www.strideout-footoil.com).

Sunscreen

Exposure to strong sunlight is not purely a risk in the summer or hot climates, and a small tube of high-factor sunscreen for the face plus a lip balm can prevent this.

Antibacterial gels and wipes

Gels and wipes now come in tiny travel sizes and if you are likely to be eating, they can ensure your hands are clean, particularly if you've had to remove muddy paws from your poles. The wipes are also essential for cleaning minor cuts and abrasions.

Insect repellent

This is necessary in some regions and if you have an allergic reaction to insect bites, these repellents come in either spray, wipes or wristband forms. Personally, I prefer the natural ones that have a citronella base.

Energy gels or bars

You never know when you might get held up and the one thing an active body needs is fuel, so you may feel you want to carry either a sachet of energy gel or a protein bar. There are many available and they do tend to keep for longer than any comparable fresh healthy snack, and can stay in your pack until you need them.

GADGETS

MONITORING AND TRACKING
Pedometers

Simple pedometers come in all shapes and sizes, and basic ones are really cheap to buy. While some people prefer gadgets that include complicated functions, it is also possible to gain a huge amount of motivation and progression from simply counting the steps you take.

However, if you're going down the gadget route, most clip to a belt or can be hung around your neck, and they record the simple movement of your steps.

Unlike the more sophisticated gadgets below, you will need to make a note of the information and set yourself some goals in order to get the most benefit from using a basic pedometer. Some work on a predetermined average stride length, while others require calibration for accuracy and they need to know your personal stride length.

Figure 11.3 Pedometer

They generally come with calibration instructions, but a rough guide is to walk a known distance (a running track or marked 1km walk, for instance) and divide the distance by the total number of steps you took to complete it.

Here are some simple tips to help you get the most from using a simple pedometer:

- The recommended guidelines state that to remain healthy we need to try and achieve 10,000 steps a day. Most people only manage about 3,000 to 5,000, and unless they are runners or keen walkers most find it difficult to find the time to include any more. Because Nordic walking helps you to walk faster and increases typical calorie consumption, it's a great way to build up your steps and reach the target.
- Set the pedometer to zero either every morning or before your Nordic walk – depending on whether you are interested in calculating a daily total or measuring each separate walk.
- Its best to record a baseline to start with – again, this depends on what you intend to measure (i.e. your activity levels or your Nordic walks). To do this, you will need to record the steps for a set period of time and note them down.
- Next, you can set yourself some goals – perhaps to increase the steps taken on your typical walk or throughout the course of a week.
- To help motivate you, remember this rough calculation: if you complete the 10,000 steps you will have burned approximately 350–400 calories, covered about 8km and over the course of a week managed approximately 3,500 more calories (depending on walking speed, weight, etc.).

Expert tip

You can turn your phone into a pedometer too with simple apps like the **Runtastic** app.

Some pedometers come with a calorie counter, but to get an accurate reading you need to provide the device with your age, weight and stride length. Don't take the cheaper models too seriously, if you are intent on counting calories.

For more accurate calorie counting and physical activity monitoring, an accelerometer or personal lifestyle monitor is a far better bet (see below).

Personal lifestyle monitors

These are the latest way to measure not only your activity levels and calorie consumption, but also sleep and general well-being. Athletes these days monitor far more than simple training data, and this trend of monitoring the body has moved into the everyday market. Sports science these days enables a sports team manager to know when a player is sickening for a cold or has exerted him/herself so much during competition or match that it might affect recovery rates. These data are collected at all times and often used to make strategic decisions even during a match, where GPS monitoring will allow a manager to assess both performance and levels of fatigue.

Similar strategies are now becoming more commonplace for individual use, although in general they don't monitor blood or urine. The better ones will track your activity and food intake (which you have to input) and provide you with reports on how you are doing via an online portal, which is updated by a small device that you wear. The device is called an **accelerometer** and it differs from the basic pedometer in that it monitors *all* movement, and can ascertain if it is at a level that will have a positive effect on fitness levels (i.e. taking you into the 'aerobic zone' in which your heart is working at a rate that will burn more calories and train your body to perform better on a daily basis).

Some of the more advanced monitors can even measure sleep patterns so that the wearer can track how the body is functioning on a day-to-day basis.

The Fitbit (www.fitbit.com) is one of the most advanced systems as it provides a choice of three types of monitor, including the latest, which is a flexible wrist band capable of tracking activity and sleep patterns. Data are loaded onto either a smart phone or computer, and there are even wifi scales that will input weight.

Step Success (www.stepsuccess.com) is a similar lifestyle monitoring portal, and the device used in this instance is known as the 'pebble'. This tiny device will clip onto shoe laces or waistband and will record steps and distance plus the duration and intensity of any activity. It transmits the data to an acti-link, which is a USB device that plugs into a computer. Each user has a personal account where they can add their food intake and calculate calories in and calories out, plus gain rewards, and match themselves against others as an incentive.

Fitbug (www.fitbug.com) is fairly similar although this system also provides you with a choice of devices. The Fitbug Air is a wireless device while the Fitbug Go connects via a USB.

The Nike+ fuelband is a stylish wristband that tracks activity in much the same way using 'NikeFuel' points as a universal way to track movement irrespective of age, weight or gender (see www.nike.com).

Health tracker watches are also available (for example, see www.timex.co.uk).

If you are serious about making lifestyle changes and like the idea of motivational information and league tables, these devices and their portals are a great way to start.

Tracking devices and GPS

For some people, the depth of monitoring outlined above is not required, and simply measuring the distance covered and the time it took to do so is sufficient to provide motivation. There are a number of ways you can gain such information – from free apps to more sophisticated tracking devices.

'Endomondo' (www.endomondo.com) and **'Mapmywalk'** (www.mapmywalk.com) are great examples of smartphone apps that provide a myriad of data if switched on at the start of a walk. They track the route covered and provide analysis of the distance and time taken. Endomondo also allows you to share this live, and measures everything from duration, distance and average speed to calories burned and heart rate (if connected to a monitor). Popular with the NWUK HQ team, it also allows you to track and talk to another user and to set up leagues and challenges. Mapmywalk plans routes as well as tracking them, and even provides data on the elevation covered. Users can take part in set route challenges and gain awards like king or queen of the mountains, and access lifestyle tracking elements like a food diary if required. You can set up a group and share routes or join in with others to compete online and measure how well you are doing.

The **Walk4life** website and app also enable you to find and plan walks and track your mileage (see www.walk4life.info/app).

Outdoors Great Britain offers the full range of Ordnance Survey maps in one app. It works even when you have no phone signal, which can be a life saver in remote areas. If you do have internet connection it will find your location in seconds and show you exactly where you are (see www.outdoorsgps.com).

Handheld GPS units

While you can now find out exactly where you are or have maps on your smartphone, the original GPS (global positioning satellite) devices are still the ideal gadget for a committed walker. One of the best makes is Garmin (www.garmin.com). The eTrex20 unit is much tougher than the average smartphone and is fully waterproof. The GPS works really well even when in deep cover, and will always help you to locate where you are and how to get back to your start point.

NAVIGATION AND METEOROLOGICAL AIDS

If you are not into gadgets, a basic compass will help you to work out where you are, but make sure you know how to use it and navigate with maps.

A great way to get the perfect map for where you walk most frequently is to visit the Ordnance

Survey website and create your own personalised map. You can choose the area covered and even the picture to go on to the front. Alternatively you can subscribe to their 'OS Getamap' service, which gives you online access to their complete range of maps. You can plot routes, add notes and photos, and print, email a friend or add to a GPS unit.

One thing we all watch daily is the weather forecast. Some sports do require accurate readings of wind speeds and dew point because they can have an influence on both performance and safety. With Nordic walking, however, the main risk is lightning. In general, the forecasts online and TV/radio will indicate if this is likely.

There are also small devices that will give you a precise weather reading, wherever you are. The type of information they provide includes:

- wind speed and direction
- humidity
- altitude
- wind chill
- barometric pressure
- compass heading
- dew point

One of the top makes available is Kestrel (www.kestrelmeters.com).

However, you can also get really accurate and up-to-date information online via a number of weather websites (for example, see www.accuweather.com; www.weather.weatherbug.co.uk; www.metoffice.gov.uk).

MISCELLANEOUS GADGETS
Waterproof phone/gadget cases

If you intend to make use of any of the above apps or GPS gadgets you will definitely need

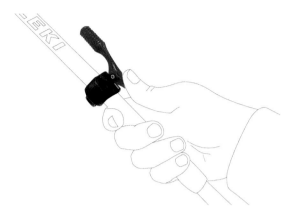

Figure 11.4 Pad butler

one of these. There are some brilliant, completely watertight cases that also allow you to access the touchscreen without taking your phone out into the elements. The best makes include Silva and Overboard.

Pad butlers

Although non-essential, this is the ultimate Nordic walking gadget. It's a small clip made by Leki that fixes to your poles and will hold your paws when you take them off to walk on softer ground.

Female comfort devices

These devices may be helpful to women who find themselves in the middle of nowhere and in need of the loo. To avoid the need to bare all, while crouching in the undergrowth, the Shewee (and similar such devices) allow you to stand up and relieve a full bladder.

Multi-tools

You never know when you might need to cut, open or even mend something, and a multi-tool will ensure you have just what you need for the job. **Note:** they are quite heavy so it's advisable to avoid the ones claiming to have every tool under the sun (for a compact range see www.beargrylls.com).

Dog harness

Nordic walking with your dog can be great fun, but there are times when your four-legged friend will need to be on a lead and that's tricky when you have poles in your hands. There are a number of waist harnesses now available that allow you to be hands-free. However, I would advise you always follow these tips before attempting to use one in order to prevent falls:

- Train the dog to stay out in front and keep moving when harnessed to avoid him/her getting tangled in your poles.
- Ideally only harness him/her once he/she has had a chance to sniff, play and do his/her business as a sudden stop could result in a complete tangle.

Well-trained dogs get the hang of the harness and anyone who has watched a cani-cross event (running with dogs; see www.cani-cross.co.uk) will know that they absolutely love it too. Some of the best kit for active outdoorsy dogs can be found at www.ruffwear.co.uk.

Water filtration system

On longer walks, it is difficult to carry enough water and yet risky to drink from streams or farm taps, for instance. That's where the new water filtration bottles come in. PurifiCup is a brilliant reusable filter, similar to that used in jugs at home, but cup-sized (see https://purificup.com). It really does ensure that you can access clean water pretty much anywhere. Bobble is a sports bottle with filtration (see www.waterbobble.com).

Waterproof notebook

You never know when you might need to make a note of something. I simply would not venture out without my trusty waterproof notebook. It really is totally weatherproof and isn't expensive either (see www.riteintherain.com).

Solar rechargers

If you are likely to be out and about for any length of time and are a gadget freak, you might want to pack a solar recharger that will ensure your precious gizmos keep performing wherever you are. One of the lightest and most reliable is the Goal Zero Switch 8.

SAFETY GADGETS

If you are Nordic walking on roads or in the dark, you need to make sure that you are seen. Here are a few nifty items that I would not be without on a dark evening.

Pole lights

Nordic walking in the dark is made much safer, and indeed easier, if people can see you and you can see the ground in front of you. These natty little lights made by Gabel, an Italian pole manufacturer, fit onto the shaft of your poles and light up the path ahead. Take care to ensure they are fixed tightly to your poles though, or they will work themselves loose and either swivel round or slide down the poles.

Flashing backpack lights

These affordable flashing lights clip onto a backpack or belt and can be found in most bike shops.

Reflective tape

This is the ideal way to make your poles stand out from the rest and to stay safe. Reflective tape is available in most bike shops or online, and it sticks perfectly onto pole shafts, and even some footwear.

Reflective sprays

You can also get permanent reflective paint sprays for metals and a non-permanent spray for clothing too.

Foil blanket

Even on hot days, it is worthwhile to carry a foil blanket because they are lightweight, yet provide enough warmth to protect a casualty or keep you warm in the event of an emergency. Often associated with the finishing line of long-distance events, these blankets can actually be life savers in the event of an incident and they take up virtually no room at all.

Personal alarm

If you are venturing out alone in built-up areas, these can be a life saver. Remember they are only effective if there are people around to hear them.

Figure 11.5 Pole lights are a great way to be seen clearly when walking in the dark.

Whistle

An old favourite that clips onto your pack (whatever size), the whistle certainly comes into its own in an emergency. I use mine, however, to signal to others in my group, and also for circuits.

Head torches

These are totally invaluable. Not only do these brilliant lamps help you to see where you are going by lighting up the path ahead, but they let others see you too. Even if you do not venture out after dark, I would advise you to have one of these because you never know when you may get either delayed or caught out when the weather closes in. Some the best ones are made by Silva or Petzl (www.petzl.com) and the features to look out for are:

- Ease of use – make sure you can switch it on quickly and easily if you need it.
- Comfort – make sure it sits comfortably on your forehead
- Bulb types – these differ, and while halogen bulbs are really bright, they do eat up the batteries. There are hybrid halogen (xenon and krypton) bulbs that are slightly less greedy, and finally LED bulbs that provide light for far longer, but are not quite as bright as the others.

- The 'beam' – most lamps come with reflectors that direct the beam, so make sure it is correct for what you want to do (i.e. light up a wide area ahead, allow you to check the ground immediately in front of you or simply make yourself seen).
- The size of the lamp – try to select one that is lightweight and not too bulky; those designed for runners are great for Nordic walkers too.

A final note about using a head torch: don't keep it on your forehead when talking to people as the beam will shine straight in their eyes. I let mine slip around my neck when in conversation.

Reflective back pack covers and armbands

Head torches will help you be seen from the front, but you do also need to make sure you are visible from behind. Respro make a brilliant lightweight backpack cover called the Hump that has caution markings on and is highly visible. You can find these in most cycle retailers. Another good idea is to buy a reflective armband or apply tape to clothing. One regular Nordic walker I know uses a flashing reflective dog collar, and it works like a dream.

WARMING UP AND COOLING DOWN

12

WARMING UP

Before you go out fitness walking or Nordic walking, it is important to prepare your body for the activity in order to get the most out of it and avoid injury.

There's no need for laborious exercises, and you should be able to teach yourself how to cover the basics in 5 to 10 minutes before each walk. Your body will thank you for it if you do, as you can see from the list of physical and mental benefits below.

Benefits

- **Increased muscle temperature:** A warm-up programme increases the temperature within the muscles used. Once warmed up, a muscle can contract more forcefully and relax more quickly.

- **Decreased risk of injury:** A warmed-up muscle is less likely to be overstretched and less prone to injury.

- **Blood vessels dilate:** This reduces the resistance to blood flow and lowers stress on the heart.

- **Increased blood temperature:** As blood travels through the muscles, the temperature rises and the haemoglobin releases oxygen more readily. A slightly greater volume of oxygen is made available to the working muscles, and so can enhance endurance.

- **Improved range of joint motion:** For most people this will be one of the most important benefits of warming up: the ability to move the body freely and comfortably through the joint movement that occurs with faster walking.

- **Hormonal changes:** Your body increases its production of various hormones responsible for regulating energy production. During warm-up the balance of hormones responsible for regulating energy production makes more carbohydrates and fatty acids available.

- **Mental preparation:** Many people lead stressful lives and often rush to get to their walking session. The warm-up allows you the time to relax and prepare mentally for the session, with increased attention on the activity itself.

Now you know the facts, these basic moves will get you into tip-top condition both before and after the session. Because Nordic walking takes place outside, a dynamic warm-up is a good idea so that you are not standing too long in the cold. The moves outlined below will increase body temperature and serve as dynamic stretches, and can be included in a slow walk if it is really cold.

Expert tip

Correct body position

Remember to be aware of your body position during the warm-up exercises – it's important to have a good alignment of head, ribcage and pelvis.

- Gently draw your tummy muscles in towards the spine to stabilise the pelvis, keeping it still during the exercise.
- Feet should be planted hip-width apart for balance and knees remain 'soft' when standing.
- When bending the knees, your weight should be back so that the knees don't travel in front of the feet. The knees should remain in line with the second and third toes.

FEET-UP WARM-UP

The simplest way to remember all of the exercises is to start from the feet up. This sequence covers from the toes to the waist. Aim for about 10 repetitions of each exercise.

Figure 12.1 Ankle roll

Aim: To prepare and mobilise the ankle joints.

Stand with feet shoulder-width apart keeping knees 'soft' and not fixed tight (preferably with poles to provide support). Lift one foot from the floor. Circle the ankle in one direction and then the other. Then point and flex the foot. Repeat with other foot.

Figure 12.2 Rolling through foot

Aim: To prepare the foot for the action used in Nordic walking, and warm up calves, shins and ankles.

Stand with feet shoulder-width apart as above. Maintain an upright body position with the abdominals engaged. Roll back and forth from heel to toe. Depending on calf length, some backward movement of the pelvis may occur when moving to heels. While this is acceptable, be aware and try to minimise this movement.

Figure 12.3 Knee raise

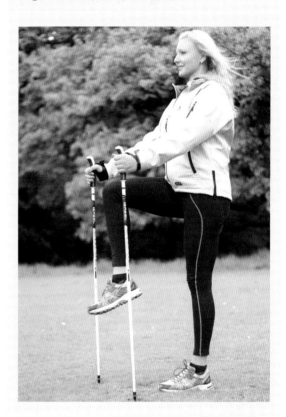

Aim: To mobilise the hips and warm up the thighs.

Using your poles for support, lift the knees alternately (marching on the spot). Lift only as high as is comfortable; the thigh should rise no higher than horizontal.

Figure 12.4 Hip rotation

Figure 12.5 Kickback

Aim: To mobilise the hips and warm up inner thighs.

Lift the knees to the front, circle to the outside and then return the foot to the ground. Alternate the legs. Work within a comfortable range of movement only. It is acceptable for your pelvis to rotate slightly if an upright body position is maintained.

Aim: To warm up the buttock and hamstring muscles.

Lift feet alternately towards the buttocks. Keep the knee still as you lift the lower leg so both knees remain in line.

Figure 12.6 Step lunge

Figure 12.7 Supported squat

Aim: To mobilise hips and knees, and to warm up buttocks, thighs (front and back) and calves.

Lunges can be conducted by stepping forwards or backwards, ideally alternating leading leg. Keep the lunge shallow, increasing depth as you progress through the warm-up. Always remain within your comfort zone – never force, strain or push a movement.

Aim: To warm up the back, hips, buttocks, front and back of the thighs, and the calves.

Ensure that the knees remain in line with the feet and do not travel further forwards than the toes. Bend at the knees and sit back to a depth that is comfortable. A squat should not cause knee pain and the maximum depth has been reached if you are no longer able to maintain a knee position in line with the feet.

WAIST-TO-NECK WARM-UP

This second sequence works the body from the waist up to the neck.

Figure 12.9 Spinal rotation

Figure 12.8 Side bend

Aim: To warm up the side abdominals and back muscles.

Keep the knees soft and the pelvis still. Hold the poles midway along the shafts as shown and bend gently from side to side, without leaning forwards or back. If you need to you could use the poles for support, but you'll get a more natural bend if you hold them. To progress, hold the poles across the chest as shown.

Aim: To mobilise the spine and warm up back muscles.

Hold your poles in front of your body, with arms horizontal. Rotate gently from side to side, keeping within comfort level.

Start by keeping your feet planted on the ground, but if you feel able, progress by shifting your weight from foot to foot, in direction of rotation as shown.

Expert tip

To enhance rotation of the spine specifically, ensure the pelvis does not rotate. This can prove challenging at first. Try placing a pole between the thighs with the pole tip touching the ground behind. If the pelvis rotates, the pole presses against the inner thigh, indicating that the abdominals need to maintain better control.

Figure 12.10 Gently mobilising the spinal muscles

Figure 12.11 Chest opener

Aim: To warm up the chest and upper back muscles.

Place the poles to the side of the feet and gently drop the hands to the side as shown, breathing into the chest. Exhale and return the hands to the starting position. Do not allow the pelvis to swing forwards in the movement by keeping good posture.

Figure **12.12** Shoulder press

Aim: To mobilise the shoulders and warm up the muscles in the shoulders and back of the arms.

Simply hold the poles horizontally and press them upwards from the collarbone to above the head and repeat.

Figure **12.13** Pole kayak

Aim: To warm up the muscles in the shoulders, arms, chest, back and side abdominals.

Hold the poles horizontally across your body. Punch one hand out in front of the face while pulling the other hand in towards the waist. Repeat on the other side, maintaining a still pelvis throughout the exercise. Repeat backwards, punching the lower hand out at navel height.

Now your joints and muscles are ready to be worked, so pick up your poles and off you go.

It's a good idea to phase the intensity of your walk. In order to give the heart and lungs the same chance to gradually work up to a higher workload it is advisable to structure your Nordic walking sessions with at least five minutes of warm-ups before gradually raising the pulse. At the end of the session, phase down gradually and stretch. This is called the aerobic curve and if fitness is your aim, you should adopt the principles outlined. As with the warm-ups, your body will thank you for it.

COOLING DOWN

After your walk, it's also important to gently cool your muscles down and stretch them out rather than stopping suddenly and jumping into the car or flopping on the couch.

Muscles are made up of masses of fibres that contract and shorten when worked hard, so it's important to lengthen them after the workout to help them to recover from the activity, and improve their condition and tone, rather than allowing them to simply tighten and feel sore. Stretching also conditions the tendons that connect the muscles to your bones, so regular gentle stretching gradually improves your range of movement, and it feels good too.

Keypoints

- Never stretch cold muscles.
- Relax and breathe normally while stretching.
- Never 'bounce' or force a stretch – movement should be gradual.
- Never push through pain.
- Have a structured stretch routine to avoid imbalance between areas of your body.
- Never rush stretches or hold for a few seconds only.

Stretching is something to enjoy and to take time over as to be effective every movement should be held for 10–30 seconds. You will soon notice that your ability to stretch further will increase over time.

The following stretches are mainly shown using poles, but they can be performed without them in most instances. I would recommend that the forward-bend stretches be performed using a support such as a park bench, wall or tree, if no poles are being used. Always engage abdominals slightly when performing your stretches, and maintain good posture and a straight back when bending forwards. As with the warm-ups, it is recommended that you start from the feet upwards and remember the sequence of lower and upper movements.

LOWER-BODY STRETCHES

Figure 12.14 Calf stretch

Figure 12.15 Hamstring stretch

Aim: To stretch and condition the calf muscles.

Keep your pelvis facing forwards. Step back with one foot and put your heel to ground. Bend the front knee slightly to increase the stretch on the rear calf. To emphasise the large upper calf area, maintain straight knee. To emphasise the lower calf, bend your back knee slightly and drop the weight back towards the heel as shown.

Aim: To stretch and condition the back of the thigh.

Keep your back straight and your head in line with your spine. Bend the back knee and place the weight on your back leg. Bow forwards from the waist. Some people may experience a more effective hamstring stretch by placing the front foot flat on ground. Another variation is to pull your poles into the top of the thigh, as shown.

Figure 12.16 Quadriceps stretch

Figure 12.17 Buttock stretch

Aim: To stretch the front of the thigh.

Place the poles in one hand and use for balance. Lift the opposite lower leg and take hold of the top of your foot, ankle or trouser leg. Bring your knees together. Maintain abdominal control to prevent the pelvis travelling forwards and creating a curve of the spine.

Aim: To stretch the buttock muscles.

Using poles for support, bend one knee and bring the opposite lower leg across your thigh. Maintain a level pelvis and sit back into the stretch on the raised side buttock.

Figure 12.18 Lunge stretch

UPPER-BODY STRETCHES

Figure 12.19 Back and leg stretch

Aim: To stretch the muscles that articulate the hips.

Using poles for support, take a large step back. Pull your stomach muscles in and tuck your pelvis under your body to support your back and initiate the stretch in the hip area. Bend your front knee to drop into a stretch. Deepen the stretch by pushing the rear heel away. It is essential the order above is followed to protect the back, hips and knees.

Aim: To stretch the back of the thighs, buttocks, spinal and upper-back muscles.

Option 1: From upright, walk poles forwards and bend from waist. Keep your abdominals engaged and your knees soft at all times. Drop your head between your arms with your back horizontal. Visualise someone pulling the pelvis back while your arms reach forwards.

Option 2: Gear lever stretch. To maximise the stretch through one side of the back and shoulders, transfer the weight on to one foot, bending the same-side knee and reaching forwards with the same-side arm. Pull the opposite arm back towards the shoulder. Gently turn the pelvis away from the stretching side.

To return to upright on both options, return to a central position with the weight evenly distributed between the feet. Pull the stomach in, push down lightly on the poles, tuck the pelvis under the body and roll up through the vertebrae. Bring the head to upright last, and finish in an upright standing position.

Figure 12.20 Shoulder and chest stretch

Aim: To stretch the shoulder and chest muscles.

Maintain an upright body position with stomach muscles lightly pulled in. Hold the ends of the poles and take the poles above or beyond the head, avoiding arching the lower back. Breathe into your chest to deepen the chest stretch.

Figure 12.21 Chest stretch

Figure 12.22 Side bend

Aim: To stretch the chest muscles.

Place the poles horizontally behind your pelvis with your palms facing backwards. Lift the poles behind your body with your arms straight. Focus the stretch on the chest. Breathe into your chest to deepen the stretch.

Aim: To stretch the side abdominal muscles.

Keep your knees soft and your pelvis still. Hold your poles at the ends and across your upper chest. Bend gently to one side and hold for approximately 10 seconds (or less if you find this uncomfortable). Repeat on other side.

Option: You may find you gain a more effective side stretch by extending your arms above your head.

Figure 12.23 Side bend with hands above head

SHOULDER AND BACK STRETCH

Figure 12.24 Back-of-shoulder stretch

Keypoint

If you do extend your arms above your head, you must bring the poles back down to shoulder height before returning to upright, to minimise loading on the spine.

Aim: To stretch the top and back of the shoulders and the upper back.

Hold both poles in one hand. Bend your knees and lean forwards. Place your free hand on the same-side thigh for support. Bring the poles across your body, keeping your shoulders down and away from your ears. Lean forwards into the shoulder stretch.

Figure 12.25 Neck stretch

Keypoint

All neck stretches should be performed gently, only gradually increasing the intensity of the stretch.

Aim: To stretch the sides of the neck and upper back.

Standing upright, gently tilt head to one side. Gently push the arm on the opposite side down the thigh to increase stretch. Holding the poles as shown will help you to concentrate on this. Very gently tilt the head forwards to emphasise the upper trapezius muscle.

PART **FIVE**

5

IMPROVERS

ADVANCED
// TECHNIQUE

13

If you have completed Part One of this book and, through practice, have fully grasped the basics of Nordic walking, or if you are already a regular Nordic walker, you are now ready to look at how you can perfect your technique.

This chapter also includes:
- Workout drills.
- A ski fit plan.
- An understanding of how to continually add progression to your Nordic walking in order to keep improving.

So let's look more at technique.

Make sure you are fully warmed up and are confident that you understand Gears 1, 2 and 3. Pick up your poles and gently run through the gears, until you are pushing gently into the strap and the hand is going past the hip.

Figure 13.1 'Squeezing' the triceps

GEAR 3+ (THE SQUEEZE)

Before you move into Gear 4, you can actually add some 'oomph' to Gear 3 by increasing the push back past the hip slightly, consciously maintaining a good forward arm swing and ensuring the pole is planted in the same position as previously taught. You should now notice

that this long swing and push back has resulted in a faster pace and good long stride. You can also now add a bit more work for your triceps (backs of the arms) by squeezing them in order to straighten the arm on the back swing.

Expert tip

Sometimes it's tempting to exaggerate your stride length by reaching your front heel further forwards and trying to almost throw yourself forwards. This is likely to create unnatural movement patterns and may result in hip or back pain, if done on a prolonged basis. Make sure you're really pushing off your toes to keep up the speed.

PRACTICE DRILL 1

Run through the gears, as before, but put more effort into every push past the hip when you get to Gear 3 – making sure you do not compromise the forward swing by checking it still reaches handshake height. Check also that you are pushing off from the toes and not simply trying to over-stride in order to gain speed.

Now it's time to work the backs of the arms.

PRACTICE DRILL 2

At the furthest point of your push back, squeeze the back of your arms (triceps muscles) to straighten your elbow. If you're doing this well, you'll feel the burn on the back of your arms in under a minute. Continuing at this intensity will be very demanding so you may need to give yourself some recovery periods between bursts of squeezing your triceps.

By pushing that bit further and implementing the 'triceps squeeze' you should have automatically noticed that the articulation in the strap has increased, and you are loosening the grip more and opening your fingers slightly at the final point of the movement. It is important to make sure you are not turning the palm to the rear as you do this or it will turn your shoulder inwards and create poor shoulder girdle posture. Concentrate on lifting the chest forwards in order to maintain good posture and a neutral shoulder position.

Having followed the stages of developing your technique as set out in this book, you should now have improved your skill, confidence and fitness, and you should also be holding yourself and moving well. To complete your awareness of good body position and movement in Nordic walking it is now time to focus your attention on your body's forward lean and natural trunk rotation. This is NWUK Gear 4.

GEAR 4

We have now covered the basic elements that make up effective Nordic walking, and what you have already learned will fall into place with plenty of practice. There is, however, one final gear that can add a further dimension to your technique – Gear 4.

By slightly adjusting your posture, you can add even **more** effectiveness and engage your core muscles more too. However, this is not essential if you simply want to Nordic walk socially because this gear does up the ante and require more hard work and focus (chatting thus becomes a lot harder).

To be able to fully appreciate Gear 4, you need to perfect natural rotation and shoulder blade movement. Before we work on the gear, it is worth spending some time to make sure that the natural rotation of your upper body is not exaggerated, but is merely enhanced by the increased arm swing and stride length.

The opposing movements of arms and legs create rotation in the trunk when you walk, and it is important to become aware of your natural gentle trunk rotation and enhance this slightly, rather than try to create large rotations of your trunk or ribcage. Your shoulder blades should gently glide around the back of your ribcage as you swing your arms; nothing should be forced. Becoming more aware of the natural rotation of the ribcage and trunk often leads to better rotation and greater freedom of movement.

PRACTICE DRILL 1: SHOULDER ROTATIONS

If you are not clear about whether you are getting the natural rotation, this drill should help, but you will need to find a partner or friend to give you a hand.

You will need to stand still for this drill, either with your feet slightly apart or with one foot slightly in front of the other for greater stability.

- Hold your poles halfway down the shaft (just as you did when you were first learning the basic Nordic walking movements). Make sure the tip of the pole is pointing forwards or, even better, place the paws on the tips.
- Ask a friend to stand behind you and **lightly** place their open palms on your shoulder blades.
- Standing still, swing your arms backwards and forwards from your shoulders. Keep your arms straight, as with good Nordic walking technique. (**Note:** you may find that your poles come close to hitting your friend. This is why you need to keep the paws on. Your friend will also need to step in close so the poles swing past their hips also – time to get cosy.)
- If your friend lightly presses on your shoulder blades (not so much that you feel like you are going to fall forwards), you should both be able to feel your shoulder blades gently gliding around your ribcage. If you can't feel anything,

Figure 13.2 A partner or instructor can help you be aware of the movement of your shoulder blades

ask your friend to press a little harder but make sure they are not stopping your shoulder blades from moving naturally.

Note: you may find that your shoulder blades don't move very smoothly or that one does and the other doesn't. It's a good idea to try this drill again a month after your first efforts and judge if there is any improvement from your Nordic walking efforts.

PRACTICE DRILL 2: WALKING SHOULDER ROTATIONS

If you and your friend are both comfortable with drill 1, you can repeat while walking. Your friend will still need to stand in close behind you and make sure that their feet are in rhythm with yours (i.e. you both step forwards off the same foot so that your friend avoids stepping on your heels).

Now back to Gear 4. So far, we have maintained a relaxed natural posture and concentrated on getting the gear right – now let's think how a slight shift in body weight might increase

Figure 13.3 Here the body weight is on the balls of the feet

the upper body workload and engage the core (stomach) muscles.

First, you will need to understand what you are trying to feel, so stand up straight with the poles in front of you.

Then, gently lean forwards and shift your body weight onto the balls of the feet and slightly stretch your upper body forwards and upwards as if you were crossing a finishing line in a race. You should feel your abdominals engage at this point.

It is important not to simply lean forwards or bend at the waist, but to consciously stretch upwards too.

Next, take a step forwards, while maintaining the lean and stretch of the torso, and begin to walk forwards without using the poles, to practise the upper torso position.

Maintain this position and you will feel your abdominal muscles engaging.

Figure 13.4 Avoid bending at the waist like this

Figure 13.5 Finish line position shown with poles lifted to demonstrate correct body angle

PRACTICE DRILL 3

Now let's transfer the body position above to your Nordic walking. Start Nordic walking gently and it should almost feel as if you are 'falling' onto the poles as they are planted.

Begin by getting into Gear 1 and then perfect the slight lean and stretch as before – feel how this engages the core with every step and makes Gear 1 feel harder. Now, go up through the gears (if you can) and ascertain which level feels the most comfortable for you. Many people find that they can manage to hold the Gear 4 posture quite well when they are in the lower two gears, but find it more challenging to hold it while Nordic walking in Gear 3.

GEAR 4 CHECKS

- Lean the upper body forwards, but avoid dipping or bending.
- Elongate the chest area.
- Check position in each gear.
- Never strain – drop back down a gear when you feel overloaded.

That's it as far as the technique variations we teach in the UK go, but you can still get more out of your poles by adding some advanced drills like running, leaping and bounding, which I will explore below. First, I need to cover technique variations that

Expert tip

Gear 4 is really a kind of 'overdrive' and it's best to add it in short bursts to begin with. You will gradually find you can keep that position for longer, and that it feels really natural and very effective.

you may see on the internet in photos and in other books. There are lots of opinions and even arguments about which is correct, but my view is that if you stick to natural movements and keep progressing you will never look back.

OPEN-HAND TECHNIQUE

You will find that there are versions of Nordic walking that replicate the hand action of cross-country skiing, and advocate a fully open hand and full extension of the arm way behind the body (see Figure 13.6). This action is generally preceded by a shorter forward arm swing to enable the walker to match their stride pattern (you will notice this in other images where there appears to be quite a bend at the elbow on the forward arm swing), but it does still require what we at Nordic Walking UK feel is over-striding. It also requires significant rotation of the upper body, which is unadvisable for those not physically prepared for such an action via prior rigorous training regimes.

Figure 13.6 'Throw-away' open-hand technique – often pushed so far back the arm is completely straight

If you are keen to train for cross-country skiing you may wish to explore this method, but please make sure you do so with a fully qualified fitness professional or coach because of the following risks:

- **Over-striding** resulting in hip discomfort, potential lower-back issues and excessive localised exhaustion in the upper leg and hip.
- **Unnatural excessive rotation** resulting in potential back discomfort.
- **Shoulder rotation** – the shoulder turns in, which closes the chest resulting in poor posture and a reduced ability to breathe deeply (see drill below to fully appreciate this).

PRACTICE DRILL

Place one hand on the opposite shoulder, and swing the free arm backwards and forwards with the palm facing the body. Feel how the shoulder works.

Now change the hand so the palm faces upwards as it passes the hips on the back swing and pay attention to how the shoulder actually dips inwards as it does so.

At Nordic Walking UK, we concentrate on maximising forward arm swing and shoulder power, and when we want to add more impetus to our walks or exercise sessions we use the progression methods and drills outlined below.

WAYS TO ADD VARIETY AND INTENSITY

Once you can Nordic walk, you will have the coordination to add intensity with these high-intensity variations on moving with poles. After that you can see how to make every Nordic walk a different workout and to keep improving by using different forms of progression.

RUNNING WITH POLES

- Walk briskly, leaning forwards to the point of feeling that you will fall. You will naturally begin to run as you bring your foot forwards to prevent falling.
- As in running compared to ordinary walking, elbows will be slightly more bent when running with poles than Nordic walking. Maintain a fairly rigid arm, even with the increased elbow bend.
- Drive through the straps to gain propulsion from the poles.
- Maintain an upright body position.
- Run as you feel comfortable: slow running is likely to retain a heel strike, while faster Nordic running will encourage a mid- or front-foot landing.
- Increase your speed as confidence grows.

Figure 13.7 Running with poles

Figure 13.8 Bounding with poles

BOUNDING

This is a much more high-impact activity, only to be attempted if you are confident about your fitness levels. Bounding uphill will reduce impact, while increasing the cardiovascular challenge.

Bounding is basically a slow-cadence run with a high knee raise on the leading leg. The aim may be to cover the greatest distance per stride or, if applying the principles of plyometrics (a technique used by athletes to work on speed and power), spend as little contact time with the ground as possible.

SKIPPING

Skipping occurs with a step and brief hop on each foot, while travelling forwards. We all did it as children; it's great to do it with poles and can be tailored to all levels. Here are a few tips.

Figure 13.9 Skipping with poles

- Skipping is like Nordic walking in that typically the opposite leg and arms are in use at the same time. If coordination is something you struggle with you may try the march/metronome technique (see page 28), or the spotty dog (see page 147). If your aim is to build up fitness or simply have fun, this may not be an issue.
- Increase intensity by increasing speed, distance of each skip or height of knee raise on front foot.

Figure 13.10 Zigzag running with poles

ZIGZAG RUNNING

Build up as for Nordic running, but when taking each step forwards, bring in a sideways movement on each stride, stepping to the side away from centre. **Note:** be careful to not step across the centre as this may cause you trip.

SKATING

- Skating incorporates double poling with a lateral (sideways) movement, similar to that in zigzag running. There will be a leading side, so this exercise needs to be repeated on the opposite side.
- As both poles plant, step on to one foot.
- Push vigorously through the straps, push back past the hip, and hop over onto the opposite foot.
- Repeat.

Figure 13.11 Skating-style drills

DOUBLE-POLING

- Use both poles simultaneously, as detailed in the drills for Gear 2 (see pages 19–20), but add more speed and power.
- Ensure your chest remains lifted and that you utilise the power through the straps.
- Emphasise the drive from your rear foot.

If planting every two steps, change driving foot at regular intervals.

LUNGE WALKING

Increasing intensity does not always mean explosive exercise, and lunge walking is very tough.

This exercise needs to be performed in a controlled manner to avoid injury.

- Keep your body straight and your back and shoulders relaxed. Engage your core and look straight ahead (not down).
- Hold *both* poles out in front and use them both together for this exercise.
- Step forwards with one leg while double poling.
- Lower the hips on the lead leg until both knees are bent at a 90° angle.
- Make sure the front knee is in line with the ankle and not pushed forwards and make sure the other knee is not too low.
- Keeping the weight on the heels and using the poles for stability, push back up and repeat with the other leg.
- Keep changing legs for a sequence of five lunges per leg to start with.

Figure 13.12 Lunge walking

While each of the above exercises will certainly add an increase in cardiovascular training, they also all offer additional training benefits such as coordination, explosive power and increased range of movement. For maximum results, mix them up.

PROGRESSION

14

Like everything you do in life, the aim with exercise is to keep improving in order to keep getting results. This does not necessarily mean working harder or feeling uncomfortable, it simply means not doing the same thing day in and day out because your body will become used to it and improvement will not be as rapid.

Progression can be added in many ways and a skilled instructor will help you do so almost without you even noticing. It is important to understand the different ways your routine can progress. At this stage, we must also acknowledge that not everybody wants to progress all of the time. As already discussed, many Nordic walkers are happy to simply be active and sociable and to gain the natural benefits of being so. However, if weight loss, sports performance or continued fitness/health improvements are your goals then adding progression will be highly beneficial.

There are four key ways to add to the workload of a Nordic walking session:
1. Working on technique.
2. Increasing speed.
3. Increasing distance/duration of the session.
4. Choosing tougher terrain.

TECHNIQUE

The whole purpose of the NWUK gear system is so that instructors can take their clients through different levels of intensity in order to gradually build-up fitness levels and skills. Any Nordic walker can adopt the same principles and the workout plans (see Chapter 21) in this book will give you an idea of how this can be done.

Even if you are quite happy Nordic walking in Gear 2, while chatting to other people, it can make a world of difference if every now and then you change gears and add a burst of intensity – within your limits of course (see 'Measuring intensity', page 124).

A good way to do this is to use landmarks such as trees or lampposts and task yourself to switch through the gears at these points. Another idea is to have a 'gear trial' route (see next section) in which you can practise staying in a higher gear and marking the improvement over time. I use this with clients who predominantly walk in Gear 2 but are working towards joining the intermediate group, who are much faster.

GEAR TRIALS

Select a route that contains a visual marker (such as a tree) that can act as your start point for the gear trial and has regular features that can also be used to mark your finish point (for example, a fence post or park gate). Once you reach this point, move up into the gear you are currently practising and want to improve. Maintain a good Nordic walking technique in the selected gear and stop or drop down a gear as soon as you can no longer keep it up. Make a note of the marker closest to this point – some clients have used chalk on occasion, but wet weather can put paid to that.

The aim is to regularly perform the trial to see how your practice is paying off. It's always good to see a physical improvement and you will be surprised at how much longer you can stay in the higher gear each time. The benefit of staying in the higher gear is that you will be burning more calories and toning more muscles, and, when combined with slower, steady exercise, boosting weight loss, too.

Alternative methods of monitoring your performance can be in the form of pedometers, route apps and so on (see pages 88–94).

TIME/DURATION

Time – or 'duration', as it is often referred to when used for fitness programming – is another way to monitor performance and add progression to a Nordic walking session.

It can involve staying out for longer on each practice session and monitoring faster bursts, circuits or technique drills. In reality, however, many of us are time poor and you may need to use another method to progress.

TERRAIN

The surface and gradient of the ground you are walking on can really add intensity to a Nordic walk and if you want fast results, the secret is to vary your routes as much as possible. We can't all add beach Nordic walking to our weekly schedule, but most of us can find a hill or incline … even if it's a man-made one.

Beach

Walking on sand is difficult because your feet sink into the surface and it is constantly uneven, which means you have to readjust your position accordingly. Although it is kind to the knees and joints because it is softer than tarmac, this kind of walking will put extra load on the Achilles tendon and lower leg muscles, so you should build it up gradually.

Wet sand is best to start on as it is more stable, but it's good to aim for short sessions of five minutes at a time until you get used to the action that will provide a harder workout. It's advisable to keep your walking shoes on at first, but you may want to try barefoot Nordic walking if the beach is safe from hazards – take extra care with pole tips though. The action is slightly different without shoes and it will feel quite hard to begin with, so build this up gradually. Sand is also great for interval training and drills because you can mix surfaces and if there are any dunes, you can add hill work, too. In fact, training on sand dunes is an effective way to boost fitness levels and improve performance.

Hills

The simplest way to add some 'oomph' to a Nordic walking session is to make sure there is a hill in your walk. Once again, if you are new to exercise, you must build your hill work up gradually because even though the poles help massively, it can be pretty hard work for those new to the game.

Start with modest slopes, then tackle steeper ones as you begin to progress. In some areas, you will not get much choice so always be prepared to take a rest if needed. Note where you do rest, and try to get a little further next time you take the same route. When using your poles you can switch the load between upper and lower body via technique or simply work on cardiovascular fitness/calorie burning by mastering the slope. In the workout plans below you will see how you can utilise hills as part of your training regime.

Other tricky terrain

Rough uneven ground, soft boggy soil and even gravel pathways can add some terrain progression, as all need to be mastered. Long grass will 'grab' your poles and interfere with your swing, but even that can be turned into a training tool. If you find long grass is interrupting your swing, you can actually stop trying to plant the poles and allow them to drag behind you as you did in the beginner drills. Make sure you really swing the arms forwards from the shoulder and you will find you get a good upper-body workout as the grass provides resistance against the swing of your arms. You will not gain any propulsion, but it is preferable to simply lifting the poles up and not getting any workout effect at all. Finally, simply removing the paws from your poles and allowing the spikes or tips to engage with softer ground will provide a little bit more resistance than keeping them on.

SPEED

Speed can be vitally important as a way of building up fitness, but it is not simply a question of going flat out from start to finish or always being the first in your group to reach the finish marker. It is the one thing that people tend to want to measure quite early on because they can feel that they are moving well and have noticed that they complete the same route a little faster each time. Speed is most effective when used in conjunction with time, maybe as intervals or in a varied training plan. A good idea is to combine slower-paced longer walks with faster, short walks throughout the week. Another good idea is to put bursts of speed into a session, maybe from one tree to another or for a set distance. Even the least competitive individuals in my Nordic walking groups loved the regular set 1.6km 'time trail' by which they could measure improvements.

DISTANCE/STEPS

Beginners always want to know how far they have gone or if they have covered more distance than in their previous sessions. Distance is a great marker, but like speed, it is most effective when coupled with time and when used in drills. By going further every session, walkers will increase the time spent on their training. Mixing increased distance with other forms of progression will get better results, so it's advisable to have one longer session periodically in which to increase the distance and other shorter routes that work on speed, and so on. Many groups have monthly half-day walks or longer adventure walks that the regular Nordic walkers build up to.

Expert tip

A good way to monitor your progress is to find a measured 1.6km route and use this to see how you improve as weeks go by.

Don't worry if, when you are just starting out, you can't complete the distance without stopping – simply note down where you stopped and aim to go a little further next time. Once you are a regular Nordic walker, the route can be tackled periodically in order to measure improvement, and it can even be used in drills. There are thousands of measured miles listed on the Walk4life website (www.walk4life.info) or that of RunEngland (www.runengland.org), which has 321 way-marked routes of 1, 2 or 3 miles (some are measured in kilometres, so check that first).

Figure 14.1 A way-marked route

INTERVAL TRAINING

Interval training is the overall description for using bursts of speed followed by a rest or set times at different speeds as a form of training. Using time, speed and distance as measures, you can set out structured drills and keep improving, although you need to be careful to not overdo things. These methods are the basis of most sports training programmes because they help the body to improve itself by challenging it and training it to use oxygen more efficiently. You may hear the term 'fartlek', which means 'speed play' in Swedish. This is a simple form of interval training. All you need to do is add short bursts of high-speed Nordic walking (up to 45 seconds) followed by a rest.

MEASURING INTENSITY

If you are trying to improve your fitness, it is important to understand how to measure the intensity of exercise you are undertaking. This is for the following three reasons:

1. To stay safe and not risk injury or ill health.
2. To enable you to measure any improvement and to keep adding progression to your exercise plan.
3. To make sure you actually enjoy the activity and are not simply making yourself feel exhausted, or in pain or discomfort.

There are a number of ways to measure intensity depending on how serious you are with your workout plan. Heart rate monitors are the most accurate as they record exactly what is happening inside your body and how it is responding to the activity. You can read more about them in the gadgets section (see pages 88–94), but the principles are simple. They enable you to understand your resting heart rate (an indicator of your current fitness), and to understand how to stay within a zone that is suitable and will provide results when exercising – known as maximum heart rate. You will soon notice how your heart gets more efficient and how to monitor performance by working it at the correct level and seeing how long it takes to recover. Heart rate monitors come with clear guidelines, but you can also find out the basic information simply by taking your own pulse.

It's best to begin by finding out your resting heart rate. Ideally you should take this in the morning before you have exerted yourself or eaten. First, find your pulse by placing two fingers (not your thumb as this has its own pulse) on the inside of your wrist (or neck if you prefer). Count the heart beats for 15 seconds and then multiply it by 4. The total will be your resting heart rate, known as your 'HRr'. The average for an adult is between 70 and 90 beats for minute – if your rate is higher than this, it could mean that your heart is working harder than average in order to pump blood around your body. The good news is that your heart will improve with training, just like your muscles, and you will notice the difference very quickly.

The best way to measure how your fitness is improving is to measure your heart rate after you have finished exercising and then when you have rested. The time it takes your heart to recover after exercise is a good indication of whether it is getting stronger, so try to measure how quickly it returns to your HRr.

To find the best level to aim for when exercising you need to first calculate the maximum heart rate, known as the 'HRmax'.

The calculation is:

220 minus your age = HR max

The total figure you get will be a good basic guide to the maximum advised level to push your heart when exercising. However, this is a rough guide only and assumes an average resting heart rate.

Without a heart rate monitor, you will also need some basic maths in order to calculate the best heart rate zone for achieving your personal goals.

Figure 14.2 Taking your pulse

The advisable heart rate zone

- **Moderate aerobic zone:** a realistic beginner's workout: 50–60 per cent of your maximum heart rate (HRmax).

- **Weight management zone:** can be comfortably maintained for longer periods and is sometimes referred to as the 'Fat burning zone': 60–70 per cent HRmax.

- **Aerobic fitness zone:** a noticeable training effect, which challenges and feels quite vigorous: 70–80 per cent HRmax.

- **Peak performance zone:** suitable for well-trained individuals as it can raise anaerobic threshold (the point at which lactic acid builds-up in the muscles): 80–90 per cent HRmax.

It is not easy to measure your pulse while exercising, and if you stop being active it will start to fall quite quickly and not give you a clear indication of the level you have been working at. You may find it beneficial to stop and take your pulse for 6 seconds and multiply this by 10.

Caution: not everyone's maximum heart rate adheres to the formula given above. If you are just starting out on an exercise routine you may find it preferable to use a simpler method like the rate of perceived exertion chart (see below).

RATE OF PERCEIVED EXERTION

Rate of perceived exertion (RPE) is a simple way of measuring your own levels of exertion by learning how you feel and how your body is responding to the effort. It does take time to get this right as in the early stages people tend to be more aware of particular stress in one area of the body (like heavy legs or shortness of breath, for instance) rather than of the total feeling of exertion.

There are two scales that are commonly used to help people to work out the level of exertion they are feeling: the 6–20 Borg Scale and the Borg CR10 Scale. Personally, I prefer to use the 0-10 version because it is easier to remember. One benefit of using this scale is that it can be easily used while on the move.

You will need to practise in order to get the level the same each time you exercise but in principal you need to concentrate on how the exercise is affecting your *whole* body – known as 'physical stress'. This is a combination of how your muscles are feeling, your levels of breathing, sweating, effort and general fatigue. Some people tend to prefer memorising the verbal description while others focus on the number on the scale in Figure 14.3.

0	Nothing at all
0.5	Extremely weak, just noticeable
1	Very weak
2	Weak (light)
3	Moderate
4	Somewhat strong
5–6	Strong
7–8	Very strong
9	Extremely strong (almost maximal)
10	Maximal

Figure 14.3 Level of exertion using the 0–10 scale

Once you can clearly monitor the level you are working at you will be able to push yourself harder within intervals or perhaps more importantly, not overdo things.

A regular Nordic walk, during which you can chat to others and maintain technique, would be graded as about 3–4 on the scale (see Figure 14.3), while increasing intensity via technique, drills, speed and so on will start to bring you into rates of 5–6. Workout walking, in which you are constantly striving to improve your fitness and perhaps include leaps, bounds or skipping, would be graded as between 6 and 8 – and a seriously hard spell of intense Nordic drills would take you up to 10. Remember, though, we are all different and the most important thing is to grade yourself and to stick to the same rates.

Good instructors instinctively measure the intensity of their clients and seamlessly ensure they are comfortable but working hard enough to get results. If they want you to use the RPE scales, they will work with you in order to ensure they understand your personal 'grading'.

Other good ways to measure intensity are:

- Obvious physical signs that you probably need to ease back a little.
- Excessive redness of the face.
- Desire to stop immediately.
- Heavily laboured breathing.
- Lack of posture and a drop in your technique.

The talk test: If you have somebody to talk to and you cannot complete a sentence without pausing for breath, you may need to ease back a little. If you are alone, try reciting a nursery rhyme or poem, and if you feel you need to stop for breath after every few words then you are working too hard for comfort and less likely to get the results you want as your technique will be poor, and your motivation will drop because it all seems like too much hard work.

RESISTANCE EXERCISES

Resistance exercises (also referred to as muscular strength and endurance exercise, or MSE) predominantly work on strength and muscle tone, but they can also be used to add intensity to your Nordic walking. In the section I will outline the principles of resistance exercise and some ways to add it to your regime and walks.

WHAT IS RESISTANCE EXERCISE?

This used to be referred to as 'weight training' and was perceived to be quite male-oriented, as it was associated with building up large muscles. These days it is recognised more for the physical benefits it provides, and indeed is deemed so vital for overall good health that the Chief Medical Officer's guidelines now state that older adults should perform it at least twice a week.

In short, it is an action that requires a muscle to work against some form of direct resistance like a weight. During this process the muscle fibres will actually be broken down, but this is not a negative process. On the contrary, by being challenged the fibres will seek to repair and rebuild themselves in order to be strong enough to cope with the demands being placed on them.

Every time you work your muscles against the right resistance in the right way, you will be training them to keep improving. Most adults decreasingly challenge their muscles as they get older and it is said that we lose about 1 per cent of our muscle mass per year after the age of 40 as part of the ageing process as well. That is why it is essential to include it in an exercise plan, although it need not involve heavy weights or grunting.

The secret is to get both the action and the weight or resistance right.

BENEFITS OF RESISTANCE EXERCISE

- It rebuilds muscles and so improves their strength and tone.
- It has a positive impact on basal metabolic rate (the rate your body can consume calories).
- It has a positive impact on bone density, which starts to decline after the age of 30 (and it's especially important for women over 40 who are at risk of osteoporosis).

Here are some suggested resistance exercises that you can include in your Nordic walking sessions, although, once again, I would always advise that these are done under the supervision of a suitably qualified instructor (minimum Level 2).

Figure 14.4

RESISTANCE EXERCISE ON THE GO

Adding resistance to a walk is fairly easy – good technique will add more upper-body resistance, but you can also try the following, although it is preferable to stop en route and use some of the other methods outlined on the following pages.

- **Weighted backpack:** Carry this or add a bit more than usual to your backpack, although you *must* make sure you have a well-fitting backpack that also has waist straps (see page 86) in order to avoid injury.

- **Ankle or body belt weights:** Avoid ankle weights unless you already have good levels of lower-leg fitness and strong joints.

A body/waist belt ensures more even weight distribution, but again it's not advisable if you suffer from back problems.

- **Pulling a partner or a weight:** Many sport-specific drills involve athletes sprinting away while being held back with a weight or parachute that causes a drag. It is really effective as a power drill and can build leg strength. NWUK instructors use similar waist belts in circuit sessions such as trek fit and ski fit. Another way to do this is by using a tyre or a pulk similar to those used for expeditions (see Figure 14.4).

RESISTANCE EXERCISE WITH YOUR POLES

Figure 14.6 A 'supported' squat

Expert tip

An appropriate depth of squat can be determined by:
- Knee comfort – this exercise should never cause knee pain.
- Knee position control – a maximum depth has been reached if you are no longer able to maintain a knee position in line with your feet, or if your knees drop inwards.

- Stand with your feet hip or shoulder-width apart.
- Contract your abdominals and keep them tight as you bend knees as if sitting on a chair.
- Ensure your knees do not travel forwards of your toes and keep knees in line with feet. Keep your head and neck in line with your back, looking forwards and slightly down.
- Squeeze your buttocks and thighs, and return to standing position.

Decrease intensity: Use the poles upright for support.

Increase intensity: Perform the exercise on one leg only. Repeat both sides.

Figure 14.7 Lunge with poles

Figure 14.8 Triceps kickback with poles

Take a large step back with one foot, so that your front knee is bent and no further forwards than your front foot. Engage your abdominals and maintain an upright body position. Bend both knees to drop vertically, no lower than as shown in Figure 14.7.

Press down through front foot to come up. Straighten your front leg. Repeat the exercise on both sides.

Variation: Try walking lunges, which involve taking a step and then performing the movement before taking the next step forwards (see page 120).

Although the poles do not provide much resistance, this is still a great way to give an extra boost to the back of your arms (especially if you are mainly undertaking Gear 2 Nordic walking)

Stand with feet about shoulder-width apart and keep knees slightly bent. Hold your poles along the shaft so they balance nicely with the tips to the front (ideally with paws on).

Bend over, keeping your back straight and as parallel to the ground as is comfortable. Hold your poles mid-shaft and bend elbows so the hands are up by the shoulders. Now straighten the arm fully backwards as shown.

Figure 14.9 One-arm kickback

You can perform this variation on the previous kickback with one arm at a time (as shown) and even use the spare pole to support you if required.

RESISTANCE EXERCISE WITH BANDS

At NWUK we use resistance bands that are specially designed to fit onto our Nordic walking poles and have special loops for either holding in the hand or looping under the feet. These allow us to perform both solitary and partner exercises. I do not advise using rubber exercise bands that require tying.

The following exercises can be done on your own. As with the drills above, it is advisable to seek expert tuition to ensure you are performing these safely. Here are a few essential things to be aware of when using Nordic walking exercise bands.

- Always ensure the bands are correctly fixed to your poles according to manufacturer's guidelines and do not use bands that simply require tying on.
- Always check that bands are in good order and show no signs of fatigue or over-stretching.
- Never stretch a band beyond the levels advised by the manufacturer.
- Always ensure the bands are securely placed under the feet when used for upper body exercise.
- When performing upper body exercise with bands in a standing position, ensure you stand with feet at shoulder width apart with the knees slightly bent (or 'soft').

There are many variations of band exercises possible but most would require expert tuition. The following pages show a few of the simplest to give you an idea of what can be incorporated into a workout walk.

Figure 14.10 Shoulder press with band

Start position

Finish position

- Ensure straps are firmly looped under the central arch of your training shoes, not under the ball of your foot. This will ensure the strap doesn't slip out from under your foot mid-exercise.

- Take a shoulder-width stance with an overhand grip. Hold the pole wider than shoulder-width.
- To increase resistance, turn the pole so that the bands wrap around the pole more times. **Note:** it helps to take a wider step when making these turns, then step back to a shoulder-width stance.
- Bend your knees very slightly (don't have them 'locked' straight) and pull in your abdominal muscles. Make sure you keep your abdominals pulled in throughout the exercise and don't over-arch your lower back.
- Make sure you keep breathing normally throughout the exercise and don't hold your breath.
- Lift the pole so that it is horizontal across your collarbone with your forearms facing forwards, away from you. Your elbows should be directly below your wrists. This is your starting position.
- Push the poles straight up, passing just in front of your nose, until your elbows are straight and the pole is directly above your head. This is your end position.
- Slowly lower the pole back in front of your face to the starting position.

Remember, you can lessen the resistance at any time by allowing the bands to unwind from the pole slightly.

- It is not advisable to bring the pole behind your neck at any time; lift the pole in front of your face.

Note: this exercise is not advised for people with neck or shoulder injuries unless being taught by a qualified instructor.

Figure 14.11 Bicep curl with band

Feet placed in band loops

Finish position

- Ensure straps are firmly looped under the central arch of your training shoes, not under the ball of your foot. This will ensure the strap doesn't slip out from under your foot mid-exercise.
- Take a shoulder-width stance with an underhand grip.
- To increase resistance, turn the pole so that the bands wrap around the pole more times. **Note:** it helps to take a wider step when making these turns, then step back to a shoulder-width stance.
- Bend your knees very slightly (don't have them 'locked' straight) and pull in your abdominal muscles. Make sure you keep your abdominals pulled in throughout the exercise and don't over-arch your lower back.
- In the starting position, your elbows are ever so slightly in front of you and slightly bent. Keep them in this position throughout the exercise.
- Make sure you keep breathing normally throughout the exercise and don't hold your breath.
- Lift the pole, flexing at the elbow, so that your forearm comes up towards your shoulders.
- Slowly lower the poles back to the starting position.

Expert tip

Remember, you can lessen the resistance at any time by allowing the bands to unwind from the pole slightly.

RESISTANCE EXERCISE USING THE ENVIRONMENT

Nordic walking can take you anywhere, and once you get an idea of what you can use in order to add some strength work to your programme, you will soon start to see opportunity in every tree, lamppost, fence or step.

A few ideas are outlined here, but the golden rule is to always follow the principles of resistance exercise by ensuring that movements are smooth, never over-strained, and take large muscles through as much of their range as possible (rather than small bouncy movements)

Many of the movements are similar whether you are using poles, bands or the environment and you will soon recognise the patterns and even the basic terms like squat or chest press. Your own body weight forms much of the resistance in this group of exercises, while trees, benches and even outdoor play equipment can help you to get the right movement.

Step-ups

These are great for strengthening and conditioning the lower body.

Find some steps, a high curb, bench or even play equipment (see images below) and you will be able to perform a range of step variations.

Follow these basic rules:

- Try to find a step that is less than 0.3m in height.
- Step up with one foot and follow with the other.
- Step back with the same lead leg first.
- Start by using the poles to support you, keeping them on the ground beside your feet until the second leg leaves the ground.

Figure 14.12 Stepping up on a seat or bench

- Use the poles to propel you upwards.
- You can place them onto the step or bench when both feet are up if you wish – this will provide stability as you step down.
- Keep a good posture at all times and concentrate on shifting the weight to the leading leg on the step up, and alternate which leg leads in order to ensure a balanced workout.
- If discomfort is felt in knees or you need to bend forwards, it is likely the step is too high for you.

Figure 14.13 Stepping up without the aid of poles

Variations: Start with poles for support and then try step-ups without them as this will increase the effort of your legs and core muscles (see Figure 14.13).

Another option is to lift the leg higher with a bent knee and to pump the arms while stepping (see Figure 14.14).

Figure 14.14 Stepping up with arm action

Press-ups

It's easy to find fences, benches and even large rocks that can help you to work your chest, shoulders and back with a classic press-up.

Figure 14.15 A kneeling press-up using a bench

Figure 14.16 A tougher press-up

Start by kneeling on the ground but with feet raised as shown in Figure 14.15. Place hands on the bench slightly wider than shoulder-width apart with your chest close to the bench – gently push yourself upwards until your arms are almost straight and then dip back down, ensuring the elbows are held outwards as shown.

Variations: Increase the difficulty of the exercise by taking the weight onto your toes as shown in Figure 14.16 – if you are not able to keep the body straight and perform the press-ups smoothly, revert to the knee version and gradually work towards this option.

Although the angle provides less resistance, it is also possible to perform press-ups against a fence or tree as shown in Figure 14.17.

Perform no more than 10 repetitions of these before taking a rest.

Figure 14.17 A standing chest/ arm press action

Dips

This is another great exercise for toning the back of the arms. Find a low bench or something similar.

- Face away from the bench and crouch down.
- Place your hands on the bench behind you as shown in Figure 14.18 and 'walk' the feet forwards – keeping the knees bent.
- Start with the elbows in line with the shoulders and push upwards until the arm is virtually straight – make sure that the elbows do not spay out to the sides.
- Gently raise and lower yourself, while trying to achieve the correct bend and full extension of the arm as outlined above. Reduce the movement should you feel any discomfort at either stage.
- Perform no more than 10 at a time before taking a rest.

Figure 14.18 Triceps dip start position

Figure 14.19 Triceps dip with straighter legs to increase resistance

OUTDOOR GYMS

These days many local authorities provide outdoor workout equipment in parks. These are a fantastic resource for the Nordic walker who wants to add some strength and tone to their daily spin with the poles. Once again, it's always best to get a proper induction from a qualified instructor in order to ensure you are exercising safely. Follow all guidelines provided and always perform the actions in a measured and controlled way, with long movements and no bouncing or jerking. You can see from the images below how many exercises can be incorporated.

Figure 14.20 Making the most of outdoor gym/ playground equipment

RESISTANCE EXERCISE WITH A PARTNER

It is actually very easy to use your poles and a partner in order to recreate the typical resistance exercise moves that usually concentrate on one major area of the body at a time. In many of these exercises *both* of you will be getting a workout too. As usual, there a few rules to follow before getting started:

- Choose a training partner of approximately your size and determine which of you is going to be Person A and Person B.
- Always stand in a stable position and limit all movement to the muscles you are working on. A split stance (one foot further forwards than the other) is often more stable than standing with feet parallel.
- All actions should be smooth and controlled throughout the entire range of motion.
- Correct breathing: breathe out under strain; breathe in when relaxed.
- Avoid excessive competition during partner exercises. Training with a partner is an ideal way to improve body position awareness and control.
- Remember to pop the paws onto your poles to avoid any spiking.
- Ideally, use two poles end to end, with one strap and one paw together.

Figure 14.21 Partner resistance exercise for the upper back and shoulders – note the grip

Figure 14.22 Partner resistance exercise for the chest and upper back – note the underhand grip

Step one

- Hold the poles at chest level, with your arms parallel to the ground.
- Keep your shoulders low and relaxed, with your wrists straight.
- Person A now needs to push the poles towards Person B's chest. Person B must try to gently resist.
- Person B then pushes the poles towards Person A and Person A will resist.

Step two

- Retain the same stance as before.
- Person A will this time *pull* the poles to their chest with elbows in line with their shoulders. Person B resists as before.
- Repeat the pulling action for Person B.
- Hold poles at your stomach level, forearms parallel to the ground and elbows close to your body.
- Keep your shoulders low and relaxed, with your wrists straight.
- Person A pulls poles towards their stomach, while Person B resists, slowly allowing arms to straighten.
- Person B then pulls poles towards the stomach while Person A resists.

Figure 14.23 Partner resistance exercise for the shoulders and upper back – note hand placement and grip

Figure 14.24 Partner resistance exercise for the upper arms – note hand placement and grip

- Person A needs to sit, stand or kneel upright with tummy muscles engaged.
- Person A then holds the poles horizontally at shoulder level. Person B places hands palms down on poles. **Note:** Person B's hands are close to Person A's.
- Person A pushes up above head to straighten arms. Person B resists downwards. Person A does not lock elbows straight.
- Person B pushes down to start position. Person A Resists as above.

- Person A (performing front arm exercise – biceps curl) holds poles with palms upwards. Person B (performing back of arm exercise – triceps extension) holds poles to inside of Person A's hands, palms down.
- Poles start low, with both of you holding the arms straight.
- Keep your elbows fixed close to the side of your body throughout the movement.
- Person A performs a classic biceps curl against the downward resistance from Person B, finishing with a fully flexed elbow if possible.
- Person B then performs a classic 'triceps extension' against upward resistance from Person A returning to start position.

Band exercises with a partner

There are also a number of ways that you can use bands instead of poles when working in pairs, but many of these exercises require skilled instruction and supervision. These pictures will give you an idea of what an innovative instructor might include in a workout walk.

Hopefully, the ideas and drills above will provide a multitude of ways for you to boost your Nordic walking experience, but if you prefer to simply follow pre-planned workouts (see below for some one-hour workouts guaranteed to provide speedy results).

Figure 14.25 These images show how bands can be used in classes and when working with a partner

SKI FITNESS PROGRAMME

15

Nordic walking can provide the perfect off-snow preparation for *all* types of skiing, not just cross-country skiing, as many people imagine. This is because downhill skiing, boarding and even telemarking all require a range of skills and elements of fitness that can be honed by training with your poles.

'Ski fit' instructor training was developed by Nicky Parsons, one of the tutors and the ski fitness expert at NWUK. She always begins by asking the simple questions listed in Figure 15.1 – and gives the answers.

Nordic walking can quickly build your general fitness, but if you add some of the specific drills outlined below you will also be able to work on the other crucial elements of fitness mentioned above. Let's explore them in more detail in order to see why working on them in different ways can help you to perform better and enjoy your skiing more than ever.

Question	Answer
What is the most important part of your skiing holiday?	The skiing.
What is the most important part of your skiing?	That I enjoy it
What is the most important part of enjoying your skiing?	Staying upright.
What helps you to stay upright?	Coordination, agility, speed of reaction and most importantly balance.
What are the most important physical components involved in balance?	Posture, weight transfer and strength.

Figure 15.1 Nicky Parsons's questionnaire

CARDIOVASCULAR/RESPIRATORY FITNESS

This falls into three clear categories:

1. **Long, slow distance:** the endurance to be active all day and ski from the first to the last lift.

2. **Tempo:** the stamina to produce more energy for longer periods so you can complete faster and longer runs.

3. **Intensity:** the fitness to turn on intense bursts of power when needed. Uphill climbs, sprints, moguls and so on.

WEIGHT TRANSFER

Transferring body weight from one position to another plays a vital role in the technique of all snow sport disciplines; without it, both performance and enjoyment are greatly limited. Forward propulsion becomes laboured, turns are less skilful, and dexterity on the skis or board is decreased, which makes accidents and falls more likely. The skills gained from ski fit training with poles can help with transfer of weight over flat skis, boards and skates as well as 'edged' skis, boards and skates (known as edge-to-edge transfer).

BALANCE

Balance is necessary for weight transfer from one leg to another (skiing and skating) or one body position to another (boarding). It is greatly aided by good posture, which provides the vital strong core and stability when in a flexed position.

Good balance is also vital for technique development and performance, which both lead to greater satisfaction and enjoyment on the slopes. A further benefit of having good balance skills is that it is an important factor in injury prevention and working on it requires the development of strong core and lower body muscles.

COORDINATION

Good coordination involves moving upper and lower body together, ensuring they work with rather than against each other. This is important in all skiing and boarding. It is also necessary if you want to execute faster and smoother techniques, turns and jumps.

RHYTHM

This is important in order to make full use of each 'powerhouse' (upper body, lower body or core) at the correct point of the technique. Good rhythm enables efficient action and smooth weight transfer in slalom turns and lead leg change in telemark turns. It also aids the correct timing when initiating a turn, especially when using pole plants downhill. Finally, it both feels and looks good when out on the slopes.

MUSCULAR POWER AND STRENGTH

Lower-body muscular strength aids balance, explosive leg action (e.g. during mogul runs), and maintaining stable postures for longer periods (e.g. grand slalom, telemark).

Upper-body muscular strength aids technique, and posture and core strength aids balance and maintaining stable postures for long periods, and allows more powerful upper and lower-body actions (e.g. during slalom and jumping).

AGILITY AND SPEED OF REACTION

Necessary for improving speed without loss of technical action and performance (e.g. racing/mogul competitions). Also important for avoiding accidents, collisions and falls (negotiating sudden obstacles/sudden changes in terrain/poor visibility).

FLEXIBILITY

Good flexibility aids performance and is an important factor in injury prevention if a fall does occur. It can only be developed through regular gentle stretching routines.

NORDIC WALKING UK SKI FIT CIRCUITS

Here are some fun Nordic walking exercises to perform circuit style. Please note these drills are designed for fairly fit individuals who can Nordic walk and comfortably manage a week's ski holiday. Please do not attempt them if you are new to exercise or have any health problems.

If you perform these twice a week with a good two-hour Nordic walk once a week, you will not only improve your overall fitness but be fully prepared to enjoy your winter holiday.

10-MINUTE WARM-UP

Warm up as usual but include the following ski-specific warm-ups:

- Down the bumps (pushing up from small squats).
- Over the jumps (pushing right up from deeper squat on to tips of toes).
- Slalom swerve (swerving hips).
- Double poling (swinging arms from the shoulders, pushing backwards in the air with your poles).
- Finally take a gentle walk on the flat, building to a gentle walk up hill and traverse down in squat position.
- Repeat slightly faster in order to raise your breathing rate and body temperature.

20–30-MINUTE CIRCUITS

Choose six drills from those listed below – vary your choice for each separate session but practise them all in order to create a balanced programme and build on all the elements.

Moguls

(Explosive leg strength, core strength, cardiovascular)
Double leg frog jumps between two poles.

Poles held upright in each hand in front of you – distance apart can be increased with fitness. Knees can be lifted higher to make it harder.

Figure 15.2 Moguls

Ski jumps

(Explosive leg strength, core strength, cardiovascular, edge-to-edge weight transfer)

Double leg jumps over two poles laid on the ground closely parallel to each other across your forward direction of travel (to avoid landing on the poles).

Figure 15.3 Ski jumps

Crevasse leaps

(Edge-to-edge weight transfer, posture, balance, leg strength, core strength)

Single leg sideways travelling leaps plus holding the balance on landing each time.

Leaping sideways over two poles lying longways parallel (close to each other to avoid landing on the poles).

Cross-country

(Cardiovascular)

Uphill jogs using poles for upper body – can increase to uphill leaps.

Traverses

(Leg strength, balance)

Zig-zagging back downhill in squat position (crouching low down, using poles for balance).

Slaloms

(Agility, rapid change of direction, cardiovascular)

Flat running through poles stuck into the ground to simulate a ski slalom course, backwards and forwards.

Skate turns

(Agility, speed of reaction, leg strength)

Quick, short, high knee steps sideways over parallel lines (pieces of rope).

Fallen heroes

(Cardiovascular, leg strength)

Burpee/star jumps using poles laid down on the ground to mark where feet should be placed during the jumping.

Figure 15.4 Fallen heroes

Telemark heroes

(Leg strength, core strength, posture, balance)

Walking lunges with poles (used for balance or held out to side of each leading leg for core exercises).

Pole control

(Rhythm and coordination)

Rapid swapping between regular Nordic walking technique to double-pole Nordic walking technique. Also swapping between using both poles one side then the other, and even using one pole between the legs.

Suggested timings for your circuits

Perform each drill for 40 seconds.

1. Perform all six drills at a gentle pace with a two-minute recovery walk.
2. Perform all six again at tempo pace (working fairly hard) with a two-minute recovery walk.
3. Perform all six again at intense pace (working very hard) with a two-minute recovery walk.
4. Perform all six drills at very gentle pace to begin cool-down.

10–15-MINUTE COOL-DOWN AND STRETCH

Gentle Nordic walk to cool down – **5 minutes** very light push through strap, arm swing finishing in front of hips, followed by **5 minutes** walking holding poles halfway along shaft.

8–10 minute stretches (as per pages 103–110) – for flexibility, to aid performance and for injury prevention.

Many Nordic Walking UK instructors offer a specific six-week ski fit programme that can be enjoyed with a group. It is much easier to work hard when you have an instructor to show you the drills and motivate you to push yourself more. Also, as the programme is progressive, it ensures that you are pushed harder week by week in order to be in peak condition for your ski trip.

COMMON FAULTS AND HOW TO CORRECT THEM

16

This section explores some of the most common technique errors that instructors are trained to identify and help to correct. Although I call them 'faults', I use the term loosely because often they are the result of more than just a poor understanding of technique or even a result of low fitness levels/fatigue. If you feel your Nordic walking technique is not giving you the results that you want, you may recognise one or more of the factors listed below and this chapter may, therefore, help you to improve on it.

The key reason that I always advocate learning from a professional is that once a poor habit has been adopted, it can compound poor performance and even cause injury, and it will also make it much harder to learn the correct way.

Figure 16.1 Poor coordination – the leading leg and arm are on the same side, known as spotty dogging or tick-tock

FAULT: SPOTTY DOGGING

(Forward motion of arm and leg on the same side rather than the opposite side)

These days, we do not mention coordination in the early stages of learning. The key reason that people fail to establish a coordinated flow of the right leg moving forwards in conjunction with the left arm and vice versa is simply that they are actively thinking about it.

WHY IT MATTERS

Coordination is key to a natural rhythmic action that gives propulsion. It also helps to keep you balanced in movement and encourages healthy rotation of the spine.

147

HOW TO IDENTIFY IT

It's fairly simple to spot by looking at your feet and hands – you will also feel/look awkward and unnatural.

HOW TO IMPROVE IT

Natural walking drill: The best way to tackle poor coordination is to simply walk and forget any arm movement – clear your mind and concentrate on your steps only, then become aware of your arms – note that they swing gently in time with the opposite leg (when you are not thinking about it or holding poles.)

Now replicate this sequence but hold poles gently and allow them to drag behind you – once again, clear your mind and when you become aware of your arms, imagine the poles are not there. Think about simply walking as above with a gentle arm swing, allowing the arms to swing to handshake height with the poles following behind.

If at any point this becomes stiff or uncoordinated – stop and start again.

Once you have mastered this try to follow the lift and control stages, but if you notice that your arms and legs have lost coordination at any time, restart this whole sequence again.

Step and beat drill 1: The common reason for this loss of coordination is that people immediately alter leg speed once the arms come into play so another good drill is to count steps to a beat and to make sure that does not change once you introduce an arm swing movement. Tom Rutlin also covers this in his technique outline (see pages 27–28).

FAULT: LAZY HANDS

This fault generally comes from the fact that people concentrate so much on maintaining a 'light grip' that they end up holding the pole with their fingertips as if it were a pencil. This often also arises from a lack of clarity about the use of the strap and articulation, and will *always* result in lack of propulsion.

Figure 16.2 Lazy hands will not allow for articulation and correct use of the strap

WHY IT MATTERS

This light grip is ineffective and does not allow for articulation or pole control. It also does not allow the wrist to remain neutral or for correct utilisation of the strap.

HOW TO IMPROVE IT

I usually ask people who are holding the pole in this way to try double-poling with this 'lazy hand' grip, and then to double-pole and use the straps as outlined on page 20. This often helps them to see how a relaxed, yet controlled grip with a neutral wrist is far more effective because it allows them to fully use the strap and gain propulsion. Double-poling with lazy hands does not allow you to move freely at all. Practise the drills covered in Gear 2 to overcome grip issues.

FAULT: NO GRIP/OPEN HANDS

WHY IT MATTERS

This is an exaggerated case of the lazy hands discussed above and is often a result of the walker being so conscious of having a light grip that he/she literally relies on the straps to do all the work. The walker does not have control as the pole swings forwards and continues to 'drag' the pole with open hands. This lack of control can result in the walker tripping over the poles because they are not being held firmly, especially in windy conditions.

HOW TO IMPROVE IT

All the drills outlined above in this chapter should help correct this fault.

FAULT: BOBBING

A good Nordic walker will stride forwards with a very smooth action that does not result in much variation of height. If you notice that you literally bob up and down as you are striding you may need to address a number of small things (outlined below).

WHY IT MATTERS

The aim of Nordic walking is to harness the energy of your whole body in order to propel yourself forwards. If you are moving significantly upwards with each step you are wasting some of this energy.

HOW TO IMPROVE IT

A great way to test of whether you are bobbing is to get a friend to stand the other side of a fairly high fence and Nordic walk along the other side so he/she can only see your head and maybe shoulders. Your friend should be able to see if your head stays parallel with the top line of the fence as you move forwards with only a slight variation with each step. If there is a marked height change between steps then you are bobbing. Video analysis is another great way to see this.

HOW TO CORRECT IT

- Check that you are not bending the knees as you step forwards, but are placing the lead leg forwards with a straight leg and heel strike, before rolling through the foot and onto the toes.
- Check that you are not pushing yourself upwards from the toes but forwards – this should happen naturally if you are gaining propulsion from the poles (see below).
- Check that you are using the poles at the correct angle in order to gain forward propulsion.
- Check that your grip is light enough to ensure the correct pole angle and also that your arm is kept straight. Any forward motion must be driven initially by your shoulders and upper body.

FAULT: OVER-GRIPPING

WHY IT MATTERS

There are four reasons why having too tight a grip on the pole is a fault:
1. The grip will negate any use of the strap.

2. The pole will remain too vertical and not facilitate any forward propulsion.

3. The stride will be short due to points 1 and 2, and also an over-grip usually also causes a bent elbow.

4. It can cause an increase in blood pressure.

HOW TO IDENTIFY IT

You may notice a lightening in the colour of your knuckles and will feel excessive tension in the forearms (and possibly shoulders and neck). You are probably over-gripping if your pole is too upright or if the tip misses the ground altogether as you try to plant the pole and swing back.

HOW TO IMPROVE IT

To correct over-grip you need to thoroughly practise all the drills that relate to hand articulation and strap use (Gear 2), or you will simply never experience Nordic walking.

FAULT: BENT ELBOW

WHY IT MATTERS

This is another really common fault that often occurs simply because the walker does not have the functional capacity to stride forwards and use the major muscles of the upper body at the same time. It can also be the result of a lack of understanding of technique or just laziness. In essence, it simply means the walker is not swinging from the shoulder and therefore is not utilising the major muscles required to gain propulsion. A natural 'cheating mechanism' is to reduce the arm swing, which in turn allows the stride and pace to drop.

Although bent-elbow pole walking does work the back of the arms, it doesn't engage enough major muscles to provide significant weight loss or achieve fitness goals. It does provide stability and when used by a relatively sedentary population is better than simply walking.

HOW TO IDENTIFY IT

A good idea is to always check your posture when walking past a large window, or you could get somebody to film you from time to time.

Look for the triangle of light between the upper arm and the side of the body, and if it isn't there, make sure you practise your Gear 1 drills because you will not be getting the full power of the poles if you keep bending the elbow. Other signs are that the hand does not reach handshake height, there is no significant swing from the shoulder and that the pole will not plant in the correct position.

HOW TO IMPROVE IT

When correcting this fault, I generally make sure that I look at the reasons why it may be occurring, and whether it is fitness or ability oriented, I gradually introduce periods or intervals of stepping up into Gear 1. This fault tends to creep up on people and they are sometimes unaware that their technique has dropped either as a result of tiredness or complacency.

FAULT: WEAK 'PLANT'

WHY IT MATTERS

In some instances the technique looks perfectly correct with a good arm swing and loose grip, but there is actually not enough commitment when planting the pole. This results in wasted energy (or a missed opportunity to burn more calories) as the pole is simply tapped onto the ground rather than used to propel the walker forwards.

HOW TO IDENTIFY IT

A great method to identify this is the pole–no pole drill (see page 22). Try this from time to time and it will alert you to whether you have become a bit lazy in your arm work. If you do not slow down as you lift the poles, you are simply not using the power of the shoulders effectively and making the most of your straps. This can sometimes be identified by uneven wear on the paws, which have failed to engage fully with the ground and only wear in one small spot.

HOW TO IMPROVE IT

Revisit Chapter 1 and make sure that you *push* into the straps when practising Gear 2 and Gear 3.

FAULT: POLES TOO LONG

WHY IT MATTERS

If your poles are too long it will affect the pole plant angle and that will in turn affect propulsion and tip engagement with the floor. It does also affect the grip and wrist angle due to the pole angle as detailed above.

HOW TO IDENTIFY IT

If you are struggling with getting a clear pole plant (especially if the pole feels like it is slipping), can't get the grip right or feel uncomfortable in the wrists, check your pole setting. Checking your paws for uneven wear and tear might also give you a clue that something is not quite right. When poles are too long the wear will generally be at the front of the paw.

HOW TO IMPROVE IT

If you have adjustable poles, try adjusting them by 1 cm at a time and evaluate the difference. If you have fixed-length poles, try to borrow adjustable poles from somebody else. You will notice a huge difference if you get this right and Nordic walking will feel more natural.

FAULT: POLES TOO SHORT

WHY IT MATTERS

When poles are too short it is difficult to gain propulsion and you will find that you dip forwards from the shoulder as you plant the pole. Alternatively you will not achieve a good arm swing because the pole lifts too far off the ground when the hand reaches handshake height, and you feel rushed into planting your poles. They will generally be too far forwards and cause the dipping action mentioned above.

HOW TO IDENTIFY IT

Often misplanting due to a short pole will result in excessive wearing at the back of the paw rather than centrally. It also makes propulsion difficult and can cause discomfort in the back due to the dipping/twisting action described above.

HOW TO IMPROVE IT

As with poles that are too long, try adjusting your poles by 1 cm at a time and evaluate the difference. You will notice a huge difference when you get the height right.

FAULT: OVER-STRIDING

WHY IT MATTERS

Your stride should develop naturally over time, but it is easy to exaggerate the stride, and the tell-tale signs such as bobbing are caused because the correct foot roll is not initiated. The legs are virtually 'thrown' forwards and that is not ideal for the back or groin. Over-striding is usually caused because you are trying too hard to maintain speed. It's common among beginners who feel they should be keeping up with others in a group or those pushing themselves too hard.

HOW TO IMPROVE IT

Go back to basics and think about the effectiveness of your technique, rather than how fast or how far you are going. An instructor can really help, so take a refresher course – you never stop learning or improving with Nordic walking.

FAULT: LEANING BACK – STIFF UPPER BODY

WHY IT MATTERS

Stiffness in the shoulder area affects the natural rotation that should occur when the shoulder is working to swing the arm forwards. It also often causes the walker to lean backwards slightly, rather than maintain good posture.

HOW TO IDENTIFY IT

This is another area that can be spotted by either filming yourself or walking past a large shop window and looking at your posture.

HOW TO IMPROVE IT

Good posture tips include making sure that your chin is not jutting forwards and, that you are looking ahead and not downwards. Make sure you can feel your shoulders working and that you feel relaxed and natural.

FAULT: LEANING FORWARDS FROM THE WAIST

WHY IT MATTERS

Leaning forwards is not good for your back; it also reduces the effectiveness of any shoulder action and affects the long arm action.

HOW TO IDENTIFY IT

Glance at yourself in a window or mirror, if you get the opportunity, because any forward lean should be entirely natural and should not affect posture. If you are leaning or bending at the waist rather than with an extended upper body and good posture (see Gear 4, pages 113–117), then you are forcing your movements and will soon begin to feel fatigue and discomfort.

HOW TO IMPROVE IT

Work on your posture, but practise Gear 4 as this long upward lean helps to stop you leaning forwards incorrectly.

FAULT: FLAT FOOTING

WHY IT MATTERS

Hitting the ground with the sole of the foot is likely to cause foot and ankle discomfort, and it also negates the push from the toes that comes from the roll through the foot action. This may also cause the bobbing problem outlined above and may shorten the stride.

HOW TO IDENTIFY IT
Flat footing will actually sound different to normal footing as the heel-to-toe foot roll is generally quite a quiet, smooth action. Flat footing will sound harsher, almost a slapping action. It will also cause short strides, excessive knee bending and bobbing as detailed above.

HOW TO IMPROVE IT
Practise the squashing lemons drill (see page 19) and make sure that on every walk you take time to concentrate on your foot action rather than the upper body. Think about heel strike and rolling through the foot with every step, and check that you do actually push off from the toes.

MINDFUL NORDIC WALKING

17

Mindfulness is a method of decluttering the mind in order to reduce stress, tension and anxiety. It requires you to focus on 'the moment' rather than the million and one things that are usually in our minds. One of the simplest and easiest ways to practise it is when walking. Being outdoors and being active is a great tonic in itself, but Nordic walking is also a particularly good stress reliever because of its rhythmic and repetitive action.

Most Nordic walkers find that they can clear their minds quickly once they pick up the poles. However, if you find it difficult to relax, it can help you to learn how to breathe effectively and focus on your body, rather than allow your mind to fill with clutter.

DEEP BREATHING

Yoga and martial arts are famous for combining deep breathing with activity, and it is easy to transfer some of those methods when Nordic walking. First, you will need to learn how to breathe deeply and effectively in order to fill your lungs with oxygen and encourage relaxation.

Figure 17.1 Take time to appreciate your surroundings, be aware of breathing and being 'in the moment'

Practice drill 1: Oxygen boost

If you want to check how deeply you are breathing, place one hand on your chest and the other on your stomach; take a deep breath and make a note of which hand moves first. It is most likely to be the one on your chest, but it really should be the one on your stomach as that means you are actually filling your lungs fully and not 'shallow' breathing.

Next, consciously try to breathe in more deeply until you feel the stomach expand, and then practise breathing out slowly. You should feel your stomach sink back towards your spine as you expel air.

Imagine you have a balloon in your stomach that inflates as you inhale and deflates as you exhale. This will help you visualise inhaling and exhaling (see Figure 17.2).

Keep practising and you will soon become proficient at deep breathing, and that means you will have more oxygen available for muscle use.

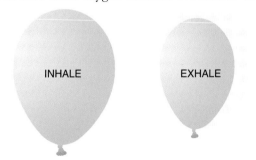

Figure 17.2 Imagine your stomach as a balloon

Practice drill 2: 4 × 4 breathing

Once you have mastered the breathing, it's time to combine that with your Nordic walking. Start by getting into a nice rhythm and pace for Nordic walking, and then clear your mind of any thoughts of technique or other external matters, and focus purely on your breathing.

Keypoint

When you exercise, your body requires oxygen in order to use fat as energy. If you exercise too intensely and breathe shallowly, you will be burning sugars rather than your fat stores. If weight loss is a goal, ease off.

Be aware of every breath you take, and gradually try to time the breaths with your steps by inhaling only at the point that you take a step at first – and then exhaling gradually as you continue to walk.

Next, try to inhale deeply and slowly as you take *four* steps, and then exhale as you take the next *four* steps.

Keep this rhythm going and focus purely on your breathing while counting your steps.

Practice drill 3: Clearing your mind

Once you have mastered the breathing and rhythm, it will all feel quite natural and you can begin to really work on relaxation. The way to clear your mind of clutter, worries and day-to-day issues is to focus calmly on your body and what you are doing.

Begin Nordic walking as usual, but concentrate more on the rhythm of the action and the way your body feels as it moves smoothly and freely. Once you have attained a good steady pace, you can begin to focus your mind.

As you take each step, while breathing deeply, notice the sensation of your feet hitting the ground, and be aware of the heel striking the ground and the push-off from the toe.

Next, focus on the muscles you are using: feel them tense and relax as you move.

Move your attention to the 'quality' of every step. Is it a light or heavy step? What is the ground surface like? Is it soft grass, slippery mud or hard tarmac? The idea is to be totally aware of every detail of the sensation of stepping and not allow the mind to wander.

Try to feel a connection to the ground with every step and feel at one with your surroundings. This may sound strange at first, particularly if you are new to 'mindfulness', but it is very grounding and allows your mind to rest.

If you notice that your attention has drifted or is becoming caught up in thoughts and feelings, gently bring it back by focusing on your feet and the simple action of them hitting the ground.

Don't worry when your mind drifts back to 'thinking' – it is natural for it to do so – but keep bringing it back to focus on the sensation of your feet moving.

Expert tip

Practise mindful walking when you have had a stressful day or you want to switch off, and you will find you that you are better able to cope. Every mind needs some down time, and the rhythm and motion of Nordic walking is the perfect time to practise this.

Many NWUK instructors offer well-being classes that include mindfulness training and relaxation, as well as balance, flexibility and gentle strength training. These were developed by the tutor Jason Feavers and can be booked online.

PART **SIX**

FITNESS AND HEALTH PROFESSIONALS

PROFESSIONAL USE OF NORDIC WALKING

18

While the bulk of this book concentrates on the use of Nordic walking as a sociable way for people to enjoy being active, it can be a useful tool for fitness professionals working in a range of different fields.

In this chapter, I outline how Nordic walking can be adapted for use by personal trainers, physiotherapists, occupational health teams, and those involved in physical activity promotion and exercise referral. Pole walking can be adapted in a number of ways and often full instructor training, which incorporates all the skills required to develop and plan group fitness walking sessions, is not necessarily appropriate.

I have had the pleasure of working with a number of highly professional individuals from a variety of fields and their expertise has helped the NWUK team create applicable training modules for their peers based on best practice. Where possible, I have included case studies and real-life examples or quotes, and indicated which form of training is best suited to each profession.

PERSONAL TRAINERS

Many personal trainers dismiss Nordic walking because they think it is either low-level exercise for older people or something that is delivered in a group format only. Both assumptions are wrong, and more enlightened personal trainers are now realising that with a pair of Nordic walking poles they can provide total-body cardiovascular work to clients of all fitness levels, in almost any location.

It is true that Nordic walking, as outlined in the technique sections of this book, will improve upper-body tone and lead to increased cardiovascular output in walking or running, but there are plenty of other ways in which a good personal trainer can use it effectively by drawing on their own skill set.

As many personal trainer clients are less inclined to go through a structured learning process that would involve low-intensity sessions, while they master their skills, personal trainers are usually advised to consider using the Exerstrider poles. This is because they can achieve whole-body engagement in a short space of time without any drills or graduated tuition. As this enables the client to get a full workout

Case study

'Growing up in north-east Scotland, we had plenty of opportunity as kids to get out on the skis, so when I was introduced to Nordic walking I jumped at the chance to become an instructor. I initially wanted to use Nordic walking to help my older clients experience a great workout outdoors without getting them jogging. What I found was a hugely versatile tool that could help them burn fat at a pace they were not used to travelling at thanks to becoming four wheel drive. I currently have a client who uses Nordic walking to recover from a recent hip operation and he now goes everywhere with his poles, including along Kensington High Street. My younger, fitter clients experience a physically tough workout when I use the poles because I can get them working as many muscles in walking as in jogging, running, bounding and skipping.'

Stuart Amory, celebrity personal trainer, London

even when first using the poles, this is far more cost-effective for them, especially when they are paying by the hour.

The Exerstrider poles therefore lend themselves to one-to-one use or small group circuit sessions as they can be picked up and put down between fast-paced drills. Having identified this use of poles by personal trainers, the NWUK education team recently developed a training course just for Level 3 personal trainers, which contains the following:

- Exerstrider pole walking and running techniques.
- Strength exercise using bands, partner drills and body weight exercises.
- HIIT (high-intensity interval training) circuits using advanced pole drills such as skipping, lunge walking and similar exercises.

Figure 18.1 These pictures show some of the drills and resistance work performed in HIIT circuits

HEALTH CLUBS AND LEISURE CENTRES

Many health clubs and leisure centres find it hard to see where an outdoor-based programme can fit in their staffing and operations, but if they view the outdoors as a further 'studio' or profit centre, it can help them to see the potential.

I really think that Nordic walking should be offered by clubs both as an option to motivate current clients (ski fit and workout walks are particularly popular with this group) and, more importantly as a way to attract those who would not typically walk across the club threshold. What better way to take a brand into a community than operating outdoor sessions? Risk assessment, insurance and route-planning issues often deter clubs from introducing outdoor exercise options, but these factors are all incorporated into good instructor training. Clubs can choose whether to train their in-house staff or employ a local independent instructor.

Participants often report that after a few months of attending a Nordic walking programme, they gain confidence in the staff and enjoy exercising so much that they do feel ready to try out the gym. Forward-thinking centres are now also retailing poles and working with NWUK to engage with workplaces, care homes and other organisations in order to reach out and help people become more active. The added benefit is that thirsty Nordic walkers tend to congregate in their refreshment areas both before and after walks.

The full Nordic walking instructor training is advisable and clubs are advised to think long and hard about the staff members they choose to deliver Nordic walking. If they personally have no interest in either the product or the types of clients it may attract, they are simply not the right person to send on a course. It is preferable to train an enthusiastic receptionist or even an existing participant than to expect a highly qualified, yet uninterested gym instructor to deliver effective, motivational outdoor sessions. This peer-led approach is key to success.

PHYSIOTHERAPY AND OCCUPATIONAL THERAPY

Physiotherapists working in private practice and the NHS have been embracing Nordic walking for both injury prevention and rehabilitation. In recent years, a wide range of conditions and injuries have responded favourably to a structured Nordic walking programme delivered by skilled physiotherapists. There is often a knock-on effect within teams for which Nordic walking may have been introduced initially as an intervention for a specific condition or particular patient, and it soon becomes more widely used.

There are three key ways a physiotherapist in private practice could introduce Nordic walking as rehabilitation:

1. Become an instructor and take clients out within their booked session.
2. Offer set sessions each week that a number of patients can attend (either with one of the team or an independent suitably qualified instructor).
3. Refer clients to a local suitably qualified instructor via the NWUK network.

Within the NHS, I am delighted to say Nordic walking is being used to treat anything from fall prevention to mental health conditions. A positive example of how extensive this can become can be seen in the St George's Healthcare NHS Trust in London, where at least 20 physiotherapists have been trained as Nordic walking instructors. Initially Nordic walking was brought in by physiotherapist Bernadette Kennedy, head of integrated falls and bone health at the trust, as part of a fall prevention strategy (see below), but its use has been adopted widely and now four core community therapy teams have attended specialist instructor training days with NWUK along with the nine exercise professionals who work alongside them.

The teams come from:
- Integrated falls and bone health – dealing mainly with osteopenia and osteoporosis patients.
- The primary care therapy team – typically a home-based community service.
- The neurological rehabilitation team – who deal with conditions such as Parkinson's disease.
- The mental health team – focusing on depression and mental health.

Bernadette Kennedy on the importance of Nordic walking

'Nordic walking is a core component of our bone health intervention programme, which is a targeted prevention stream focusing on adults who have a diagnosis of osteopenia or osteoporosis but who are not yet at high risk of falling – as if this population do become at risk of falling they will have a significantly higher risk of fracture than the rest of the population. The core component of our Nordic walking programme is focused on bone loading and strength training activities, but equally balance activities can be weaved into the sessions to ensure that a full and varied prevention programme is in place – addressing strength, power, coordination, balance and bone loading. Nordic walking provides the opportunity to embrace the core prevention programme outdoors, providing the additional opportunity for Vitamin D production during the summer months.

The other arm of our service focuses on the falls population (those mainly over 65 who have fallen in the past year or are at risk of falling).

This population would never move straight into Nordic walking – they are not active enough to participate safely in Nordic walking and the focus for this population is always stability first and then progressing onto mobility once any reversible risk factors for falls have been addressed. Nordic walking may well be a step-up option, along with other exercise activities for maintaining and progressing mobility.

There are many opportunities to integrate Nordic walking instructors and indeed other exercise instructors into health provider teams to ensure that the prevention of falls and fractures and the appropriate management of any falls/fracture risk is implemented to meet the needs of individual patients. Within my team now we have five exercise instructors, 10+ physiotherapists and two occupational therapists.'

Bernadette Kennedy is a chartered physiotherapist and head of integrated falls and bone health, St George's Healthcare NHS Trust

Figure 18.2 The St George's physiotherapy team have embraced Nordic walking

The delivery process of Nordic walking at St George's has been adapted according to the conditions being treated by each team. The bone health team offer tuition and induction over a four to six-week period in a group format of usually four to five patients per instructor. They then issue Freedom Cards and the participants are able to join in regular walks that are led by qualified walk leaders, either rehab assistants or trained from within the group. The centre offers seven social walks every week in a range of locations in south London and at varying times in order to maximise attendance. They also provide a pole hire service and ensure they regularly attend the groups to provide support and progression.

The neurological team offer a longer induction period as they need to match the patients' specific needs (many have Parkinson's disease) and tailor the programmes accordingly.

The National Ankylosing Spondylitis Society in the UK have been so impressed with their recent trials that they are working with NWUK to set up exercise sessions for their groups across the UK. The trial group based in Yeovil, Somerset, attended a seven-week programme with Level 4 instructor Helen Gilchrist, using Nordic walking as their primary exercise. Helen also introduced flexibility exercises, intervals and band work in order to encompass all of the key elements recommended for sufferers of the condition. Working with the group's physiotherapist (Sue Chesterman), Helen wanted to help the patients improve the following:

- Range of movement in joints.
- Posture control.
- Muscle strength.
- Muscle length.
- Lung capacity.
- Balance.
- Cardiovascular fitness.

The group members were all surprised at how noticeable their improvements were, especially those who had hip replacements or spinal curvatures due to their condition. One participant commented that he usually stares at the ground when walking, but the poles helped him to look ahead.

CANCER REHABILITATION UNITS

Nordic walking has also proved beneficial for those recovering from cancer, particularly breast cancer, as the gentle shoulder action aids both lymphoedema and mobilisation, following surgery. The Ladybird Unit in Poole Hospital, Dorset, has used Nordic walking as part of its treatment for nearly five years, and it provides access to regular walks via a local instructor and also leaders trained from within the group. This 'peer-led' approach has significant benefits to both newcomers and those who have already completed the programme and feel able to provide support to others.

EXERCISE REFERRAL AND RECOMMENDATION

As already outlined in the health section, Nordic walking provides an exercise format that can benefit a number of NCDs (non-communicable diseases) and it can be integrated easily into exercise referral programmes. While these have traditionally been 12-week interventions based primarily in fitness centres, there is great scope for the exercise to be taken to the participants, rather than expecting them to attend what can seem intimidating environments.

Many such schemes operate across the UK and the results from where a Nordic walking option has been provided have been impressive. However, there is scope for more adoption of such programmes. The recent development of the UK's first bespoke exercise referral qualification, which uses walking as the primary intervention, is the first step towards this. NWUK developed this bespoke course because many instructors have entered the 'fitness industry' with a desire to encourage well-being. We have been delighted at the response from practice nurses and others who work within the health sector, and have identified the simplicity of using Nordic walking to both prevent and manage conditions that are physically and emotionally costly to us all.

Our mission is to build a network of highly qualified professionals who can deliver programmes in their locality and provide GPs with a simple solution that can be offered from the surgery door.

One major project that has used innovation and Nordic walking has been in operation on the east coast of the UK for over three years. Charles Allen and his team from the East Coast Community Healthcare Physical Activity Team operate a 'hub' system across a vast area, spanning over 482km in the largely rural area around Great Yarmouth and Norwich.

Participants are referred initially to the 'hubs' for specialist exercise advice and evaluation, and then sign-posted to a range of activities in the locality. Where possible, Nordic walking is used because it enables the participants to access regular exercise while under the guidance of the team in the hub, and also in the longer term once they have graduated. There are 12 specialist physical activity instructors, trained to deliver Nordic walking as part of the referral process. They work to different client-to-instructor ratios, depending on the medical conditions and needs of each participant. This varies from 1:1 to 1:8.

There are at least 12 community walks per week. The team will accompany referred patients, and plans are afoot to offer the hub services from local pharmacies, too. Up to 140 people attend walks each week and the team have calculated that 2 out of every 3 people introduced to Nordic walking have increased activity levels (based on self-efficacy information) and are recorded as having attended community walks within every 3-month evaluation period. They also have evidence that over 50 of the 432 original referred patients also Nordic walk independently. They are now working with the University of East Anglia and a study of 160 participants will evaluate the effectiveness of both indoor and outdoor exercise referral protocols over a two-year period.

Charles Allen on Nordic walking

'Nordic walking is seen as a key factor in tackling ill health by the East Coast Community Healthcare Physical Activity Team. I love the product and think it should be adopted by all NHS teams because:

- Nordic walking allows the inactive and medically constrained to improve their health.
- Nordic walking has allowed specialist physical activity instructors to offer patients a method to stay physically active past intervention.
- Nordic walking is a fantastic way for people to address all five components of fitness and reach the Chief Medical Officer's recommendations of 150 minutes of moderate physical activity.

I have been working with stroke/aneurysm patients and use Nordic walking as a major part of the rehabilitation process from week 4 onwards. I think that Nordic walking prevents blood pooling as systolic pressure remains more consistent than walking without poles. I also feel that improved posture and awareness of movement patterns are particularly useful in the rehabilitation of mild stroke and aneurysm patients who are mobile.

Finally, I have been trying some static muscle release using poles, which reduces joint pain and increases ROM.'

Charles Allen is owner of Active Lives and exercise referral specialist with East Coast Community Healthcare

The team also use Nordic walking in schools and have found that the less 'sporty' children often gain confidence from mastering a skill that none of their peers have experienced.

Current exercise referral instructors would require the two-day instructor-training programme and would also benefit from the well-being modules that include training on how to adapt Nordic walking for the elderly and those with certain physical and mental conditions. The Nordic and fitness walking-specific exercise referral diploma is available for any instructor who has completed both the NWUK initial training and a minimum Level 2 fitness qualification.

WORKPLACE AND OCCUPATIONAL HEALTH

This is an area in which the use of Nordic walking has grown rapidly in the past couple of years, and one that I find very exciting. Forward-thinking organisations provide low-cost gym membership and other incentives for their employees because they recognise that a sedentary workforce is more likely to take sick leave and have increased levels of long-term ill health. Nordic walking can, in essence, mean that every employee has access to a cross-training machine at a fraction of the cost of installing a gym or subsidising member-ships. Nordic walking can be far more than a physical activity programme. In pilot schemes, we have seen how it has helped employees bond as teams and even enabled them to have active meetings.

A 20–30-minute Nordic walk at lunchtime is really energising and ticks all the boxes as far as physical activity guidelines are concerned. It is great for those who sit at computers all day, and the equipment and delivery costs are minimal. Another benefit is that those who take up Nordic walking at work often also join a group closer to home for evening and weekend exercise with family and friends.

NWUK now manage a number of workplace schemes where delivery partner instructors have been deployed to visit regularly in order to host 'Learn to Nordic walk' courses for newcomers and to supervise in-house leaders who help to both plan and promote a range of walks for all levels.

In other organisations, an employee has been trained to take on the role of the instructor, and in these instances we provide further training to enable the individual to also train walk leaders internally. This enables him/her to ensure that there are safe regular walks on offer. Large organisations will have dedicated occupational health teams who can help to implement such programmes, but smaller organisations can also set up such schemes and encourage each other to get in those vital minutes of physical activity during the working week. Other companies encourage employees to Nordic walk to and from the workplace.

Workplace health 'packages', providing a complete solution (training, equipment and promotion) that can be scaled up according to the number of employees, have been really effective.

Case study: Moors Valley Country Park, East Dorset

Moors Valley Country Park is a great example of how a visitor attraction run jointly by the Forestry Commission and the local authority (East Dorset District Council) has become a major player in the drive to get local people active. Moors Valley has been a NWUK centre of excellence for several years. To date, it has recorded nearly 8,000 attendees to its Nordic walking sessions, held 8 times a week (over a 3-year period). The team of 9 instructors run 20 'Learn to Nordic walk' courses a year in four locations, including the park. It offers a full NWUK programme of well-being, adventure and workout walks for all abilities, and even has a GP referral specialist who works one-to-one with people who need that level of care due to health issues.

Karl Prince, one of the healthy lifestyle rangers based at the park, says:

'Nordic walking is a fantastic activity for people of all ages and abilities, as it makes something we can all do twice as effective. Over 600 individuals have trained in Nordic walking through the programme offered by East Dorset District Council and 82% have gone on to Nordic walk, in some capacity, on a weekly basis.'

ACTIVITY PROMOTION: COMMUNITY ENGAGEMENT

Local authorities, sports partnerships and even some NHS trusts across the UK have implemented Nordic walking schemes designed primarily to attract the less active in the community. These are generally low-cost solutions, with equipment for hire. The use of volunteer walk leaders has also grown impressively. While these schemes tended to be aimed at the over-50s in the first instance, many have expanded their remit and now offer workplace health solutions for local companies, and weekend and evening sessions aimed at the younger adult, too.

They tend to use a mixture of in-house staff and external freelance instructors, and they are certainly not only in leafy areas. Age UK Newham, in central London, offers inspirational sessions in primarily urban locations that have been growing in popularity year on year since 2008. Other projects around the UK are recording high participation levels and good rates of retention.

Here are a just a few examples:

- Active Walks Sefton, in the north-west, record as many as 124 Nordic walkers attending walks each week.
- Northamptonshire Sports Partnership taught over 200 people to Nordic walk in the first year of its project and now operates right across the county with a network of volunteer walk leaders.
- Tone Leisure in Somerset has issued over 200 NWUK Freedom Cards in its first year and is expanding into rural areas in a bid to get local villages active.

CARE HOMES

Pole walking has the potential to be one of the most effective forms of exercise provision for the elderly in retirement complexes and care homes. Tom Rutlin has pioneered its use in the US, and a pilot by Peggy Buchanan at a retirement complex in California focused on residents with an average age of 87, who agreed to trade in their single canes

Peggy Buchanan on the benefits of Nordic walking for the elderly

'People with canes and walkers tend to see themselves as "invalids", but the same people with walking poles more often feel like "athletes". Those who traded in walkers immediately began walking with a more upright posture and their gait pattern went from the "walker shuffle" to a more normal walking gait – and the psychological benefits may have been as important as the physical benefits. Participants walked with greater confidence and a smile of satisfaction on their faces. Those who traded their single canes for a pair of the poles immediately felt the benefit of an additional point in contact with the ground and using the poles quickly began to correct the leaning that generally comes with cane use.'

Peggy Buchanan, coordinator of vitality/wellness programming, Vista del Monte retirement community, Santa Barbara, California

or frame walkers for a pair of Exerstrider poles for a period of 13 weeks. The results were impressive and led to the development of Rutlin's innovative 'stability for mobility' programme that takes seniors through a sit-to-stand-to-walk sequence. Where this concept has been introduced, residents now regularly use poles as a way to walk around the complex and poles are made available at every doorway.

In the UK, the sit-to-stand sequence has been bolted on to a well-being programme that incorporates balance, strength and flexibility drills designed to encourage mobility and independence into older age. This programme is available in a one-day training course for those working within the care sector.

RUNNING AND SPORTS COACHES

Nordic walking advanced technique provides perfect cross training for a number of sports. Cyclists, for instance, can experience significant cardiovascular conditioning while working the legs at a much lower intensity than usual, and this whole-body concept that does not fatigue any major muscle group above others is equally suitable for most sports participants. It can be used effectively for both for conditioning and rehabilitation.

One of the most significant uses is by running coaches. First of all it can be used as a tool for helping the deconditioned who wish to take up jogging, and also as rehabilitation for injured runners desperate to keep their cardiovascular fitness without compounding over-use injuries of the hips, knees and feet.

One of my major concerns recently has been how the popularity of running has led to a massive increase in beginners, who literally refuse to walk before they can run. They take to the streets and punish their joints with poor technique and gait, which causes joint overload, often compounded by excess weight and lack of general conditioning. The inevitable happens: they get injured and give up. While many running clubs do now offer supportive tuition for these beginners, it is hard to keep them motivated if you insist that they walk rather than run in the early days. Recent trials of a 'walk to run' pilot using Nordic walking enabled the coach to build up cardiovascular fitness, provide a feeling of achievement and work on the phases of good running technique ('drive, pull and lift' phases), all using pole drills. The participants all reported that they felt as if they were exercising from day one and that once they made the transition from poles to running, they had increased their fitness levels and felt ready to run.

The coaches also found that poles were a usual tool for coaching and rehabilitating other runners in the group and that their attitudes to the use of poles changed massively once they had experienced how much effort it actually required.

SKI INSTRUCTORS

Many ski instructors think that Nordic walking is only suitable as a training regime for those that prefer the cross-country tracks rather than downhill skiing or snowboarding. A quick perusal of Chapter 15 of this book will highlight how many key elements of good performance can be honed with a pair of poles and some Nordic walking drills.

Apart from providing stamina, strength, balance and weight transfer drills, it really does appeal to the committed outdoor sports enthusiast and is well worth looking into as a way to prepare for the slopes.

Ski instructors may also benefit from taking the full CYQ two-day qualification, as this will provide entry to the register of exercise professionals and consolidate their skills with the principles of fitness and safe delivery of fitness tuition (see www.cyq.org.uk).

RESEARCH INTO THE BENEFITS OF // NORDIC WALKING

19

Pole walking has been the subject of studies since the late 1980s, and these vary from very sport-specific cardiovascular output comparisons to well-being applications for the elderly or those with conditions such as Parkinson's disease.

There have also been a number of systematic reviews of the available research, and both these and the individual research studies are listed below for readers who want to find more in-depth information about Nordic walking. Where possible, the main subject area is given to help those with a specific area of interest to locate relevant information.

The research varies considerably in the positivity of results. It is always important to remember that, as we have explored in this book, there are a number of ways to deliver pole walking, and therefore a number of factors that would lead to a comprehensive study. With that in mind, it is also important to consider the following factors when evaluating research conclusions:

1. How long was the study?
2. What was group size?

The smaller the population size in study, the greater any difference found between groups must be in order to be accepted as significant.

3. Was careful consideration of technique employed?
4. Was effective Nordic walking tuition provided via suitably qualified instructors?

For instance, one study, conducted over an 8-week period in which only 27 participants completed the process, concluded that there was no significant enhancement of health benefits over ordinary walking,* but I am confident that with a larger control group, structured tuition programme, graded technique evaluation (such as the NWUK gear system outlined in this book) and a longer duration the results are likely to be significantly different.

Other studies are clearly measuring the loading of lower extremities in relation to the more intensive techniques often found in Europe. I think there is scope for more research into both the effectiveness of Nordic walking for specific conditions and how it encourages behaviour change and mental well-being, but I am encouraged by some really positive recent publications and interest from researchers.

---

*Although the same study (Knowles *et al.* 2012) did mention that there was a significant reduction in diastolic pressure (see page 173 for full reference).

SYSTEMATIC REVIEWS OF RESEARCH AVAILABLE

Fritschi, J. O., Brown, W. J., Laukkanen, R., and van Uffelen, J. G. Z. (2012) 'The effects of pole walking on health in adults: A systematic review'. *Scandinavian Journal of Medicine and Science in Sports* 22: e70–e78.

Laukkanen, R. (2007) 'Review: Scientific evidence on Nordic walking'. Available online.

Morgulec-Adamowicz, N., Marszałek, J., and Jagustyn, P. (2011) 'Nordic walking: A new form of adapted physical activity (a literature review)'. *Human Movement* 12(2): 124–32.

Tschentscher, M., Niederseer, D., and Niebauer, J. (2013) 'Health benefits of Nordic Walking – a systematic review'. *American Journal of Preventive Medicine* 44(1): 76–84.

RESEARCH RELATING TO MEDICAL CONDITIONS OR CIRCUMSTANCES

Arthritis, fibromyalgia, back pain

Anttila, M. A., Holopainen, T., and Jokinen, S. (1999) 'Polewalking and the effect of regular 12-week polewalking exercise on neck and shoulder symptoms, the mobility of the cervical and thoracic spine and aerobic capacity'. Final project work for the Helsinki IV (College for Health Care Professionals).

Hartvigsen, J., and Christensen, K. (2007) 'Active lifestyle protects against incident low back pain in seniors: A population-based 2-year prospective study of 1387 Danish twins aged 70–100 years'. *Spine* 32(1): 76–81.

Henkel, J., Bak, P., Otto, R., and Smolenski, U. C. (2009) 'Effect of selected prevention concepts on functional health of persons with nonspecific chronic recurrent neck pain'. *Manuelle Medizin* 47(1): 57–66.

Jones, K. D. (2011) 'Nordic walking in fibromyalgia: A means of promoting fitness that is easy for busy clinicians to recommend'. *Arthritis Research and Therapy* 13: 103.

Mannerkorpi, K., Nordeman, L., Cider, A., and Jonsson, G. (2010) 'Does moderate-to-high-intensity Nordic walking improve functional capacity and pain in fibromyalgia? A prospective randomized controlled trial'. *Arthritis Research and Therapy* 12(5): R189.

Strömbeck, B., Ekdahl, C., Manthorpe, R., Wikström, I., and Jacobsson, L. (2000) 'Health-related quality of life in primary Sjögren's syndrome, rheumatoid arthritis and fibromyalgia compared to normal population data using SF–36'. *Scandinavian Journal of Rheumatology* 29: 20–8.

Heart disease

Breyer, M. K., Breyer-Kohansal, R., Funk, G. C., Dornhofer, N., Spruit, M. A., Wouters, E. F. M., Burghuber, O. C., and Hartl, S. (2010) 'Nordic walking improves daily physical activities in COPD: A randomised controlled trial'. *Respiratory Research* 11(1): 112.

Collins, E. G., Langbein, W. E., Orebaugh, C., Bammert, C., Hanson, K., Reda, D., Edwards, L. C., and Littooy, F. N. (2005) 'Cardiovascular training effect associated with polestriding exercise in patients with peripheral arterial disease'. *Journal of Cardiovascular Nursing* 20(3): 177–85.

Jastrzebski, D., Ochman, M., Ziora, D., Labus, L., Kowalski, K., Wyrwol, J., Lutogniewska, W., Maksymiak, M., Ksiazek, B., Magner, A., Bartoszewicz, A., Kubicki, P., Hydzik, G., Zebrowska, A., and Kozielski, J. (2013). 'Pulmonary rehabilitation in patients referred for lung transplantation'. *Advances in Experimental Medicine and Biology* 755: 19–25.

Keast, M. L., Slovinec D'Angelo, M. E., Nelson, C. R. M, Turcotte, S. E., McDonnell, L. A., Nadler, R. E., Reed, J. L., Pipe, A. L., and Reid, R. D. (2013) 'Randomized trial of Nordic walking in patients with moderate to severe heart failure'. *Canadian Journal of Cardiology* 29(11): 1470–6.

Kocur, P., Deskur-Smielecka, E., Wilk, M., and Dylewicz, P. (2009) 'Effects of Nordic walking training on exercise capacity and fitness in men participating in early, short-term inpatient cardiac rehabilitation after an acute coronary syndrome: A controlled trial'. *Clinical Rehabilitation* 23(11): 995–1004.

Spafford, C., Oakly, C., and Beard, C. (2012) 'Availability of supervised exercise programs and the role of structured home-based exercise in peripheral arterial disease'. *European Journal of Vascular and Endovascular Surgery* 44(6): 576.

Walter, P. R., Porcari, J. P., Brice, G., and Terry, L. (1996) 'Acute responses to using walking poles in patients with coronary heart disease'. *Journal of Cardiopulmonary Rehabilitation* 16(4): 245–50.

Elderly people

Chomiuk, T., Folga, A., and Mamcarz, A. (2012) 'The influence of systematic pulse-limited physical exercise on the parameters of the cardiovascular system in patients over 65 years of age'. Third Department of Internal Medicine and Cardiology, Medical University of Warsaw, Poland.

Figueiredo, S., Finch, L., Jiali, M., Ahmed, S., Huang, A., and Mayo, N. E. (2013) 'Nordic walking for geriatric rehabilitation: A randomized pilot trial'. *Disability and Rehabilitation* 35(12): 968–75.

Koskinen, J., Kärki, M., and Virtanen, M. (2003) 'Power and balance fron Nordic walking: Effects of regular NW to muscular strength and postural control of ageing employees who are unaccustomed to regular physical exercise'. Helsinki Polytechnic Health Care and Social Services, Helsinki, Finland.

Luoma-Aho, M. (2002) 'Effects of supervised Nordic walking on physical performance in elderly men and women living in sheltered houses'. Department of Health Sciences, University of Jyväskylä, Finalnd.

Mikalacki, M., Cokorilo, N., and Katiæ, R. (2011) 'Effect of Nordic walking on functional ability and blood pressure in elderly women'. *Collegium Antropologicum* 35(3): 889–94.

Parkatti, T., Perttunen, J., and Wacker, P. (2012) 'Improvement in functional capacity from Nordic walking: A randomized-controlled trial among elderly people'. *Journal of Aging and Physical Activity* 20(1): 93–105.

Takeshima, N., Islam, M. M., Rogers, M. E., Rogers, N. L., Sengoku, N., Koizumi, D., Kitabayashi, Y., Imai, A., and Naruse, A. (2013) 'Effects of Nordic walking compared to convential walking and band-based resistance exercise on fitness in older adults'. *Journal of Sports Science and Medicine* 12(3): 422–30.

Turk, Z., Vidensek, S., and Micetic Turk D. (2007) 'Nordic walking: A new form of activity in the elderly'. *Acta Medica Croatica* 61 (supplement 1): 33–6.

Balance

Baatile, J., Langbein, W. E., Weaver, F., Maloney, C., and Jost, M. B. (2000) 'Effect of exercise on perceived quality of life of individuals with Parkinson's disease'. *Journal of Rehabilitation*

Research and Development 37(5): 529–34.

Bassett, S., Stewart, J., and Giddings, L. (2012) 'Nordic walking versus ordinary walking for people with Parkinson's disease: A single case design'. *New Zealand Journal of Physiotherapy* 40(3): 117–22.

Ebersbach, G., Ebersbach, A., Edler, D., Kaufhold, O., Kusch, M., Kupsch, A., and Wissel, J. (2010) 'Comparing exercise in Parkinson's disease: The Berlin LSVT®BIG study'. *Movement Disorders* 25(12): 1902–8.

Fritz, B., Rombach, S., Godau, J., Berg, D., Horstmann, T., and Grau, S. (2011) 'The influence of Nordic walking on sit to stand transfer in Parkinsons patients'. *Gait Posture* 34(2): 234–8.

Karinkanta, S., Heinonen, A., Sievänen, H., Uusi-Rasi, K., Pasanen, M., Ojala ,K., Fogelholm, M., and Kannus, P. (2007) 'A multi-component exercise regimen to prevent functional decline and bone fragility in home-dwelling elderly women: Randomized, controlled trial'. *Osterporosis International* 18: 453–62.

Reuter, I., Mehnert, S., Leone, P., Kaps, M., Oechsner, M., and Engelhard, M. (2011) 'Effects of a flexibility and relaxation programme, walking, and Nordic walking on Parkinson's disease'. *Journal of Aging Research* 2011, article ID 232473.

van Eijkeren, F. J., Reijmers, R. S., Kleinveld, M. J., Minten, A., Bruggen, J. P., and Bloem, B. R. (2008) 'Nordic walking improves mobility in Parkinson's disease'. *Movement Disorders* 23: 2239–43.

Diabetes

Fritz, T., Caidahl, K., Krook, A., Lundström, P., Mashili, F., Osler, M., Szekeres, F. L., Östenson, C. G., Wändell, P., and Zierath, J. R. (2013) 'Effects of Nordic walking on cardiovascular risk factors in overweight individuals with type 2 diabetes, impaired or normal glucose tolerance'. *Diabetes/Metabolism Research and Reviews* 29(1): 25–32.

Gram, B., Christensen, R., Christiansen, C., and Gram, J. (2010) 'Effects of Nordic walking and exercise in type 2 diabetes mellitus: A randomized controlled trial'. *Clinical Journal of Sport Medicine* 20(5): 355–61.

Sossai, P., Sudano, M., Caniglia, C., and Amenta, F. (2013) 'Effect of Nordic walking in type 2 diabetes mellitus: Some considerations'. *Journal of Sports Medicine and Physical Fitness* 53(3): 336–7.

Obesity

Fiqard-Fabre, H., Fabre, N., Leonardi, A., and Schema, F. (2011) 'Efficacy of Nordic Walking in Obesity Management'. *International Journal of Sports Medicine* 32: 407–14.

Venojärvi, M., Wasenius, N., Manderoos, S., Heinonen, O. J., Hernelahti, M., Lindholm, H., Surakka, J., Lindström, J., Aunola, S., Atalay, M., and Eriksson, J. G. (2013) 'Nordic walking decreased circulating chemerin and leptin concentrations in middle-aged men with impaired glucose regulation'. *Annals of Medicine* 45(2): 162–70.

Inactivity

Kortmann, T., and Schumacher, G. (2013) 'Physical activity in obesity and overweight'. *Therapeutische Umschau* 70(2): 113–7.

Kukkonen-Harjula, K., Mänttäri, A,. Hiilloskorpi, H., Pasanen, M. Laukkanen, R., Suni, J., Fogelhom, M., and Parkkari, J. (2004) 'Training responses of brisk walking with or without poles in a randomized controlled trial with middle-aged women'. 9th Annual Congress of the European College of Sport Science, Clermont-Ferrand, France.

Wanner, M., Martin-Diener, E., Bauer, G. F., Stamm, H., and Martin, B. W. (2011) 'Allez hop a nationwide programme of the promotion of physical activity: what is the evidence for a population impact after one decade of implementation?' *British Journal of Sports Medicine* 45(15): 1202–7.

Mental health

Stoughton, L. J. (1992) 'Psychological profiles before and after 12 weeks of walking or exerstrider training'. Thesis, University of Wisconsin.

Suija, K., Pechter, U., Kalda, R., Tähepõld, H., Maaroos, J., and Maaroos, H. I. (2009) 'Physical activity of depressed patients and their motivation to exercise: Nordic walking in family practice'. *International Journal of Rehabilitation Research* 32(2): 132–8.

Cancer

Leibbrand, B., Kähnert, H., Exner, A. K., Biester, I., Koller, B., Niehues, C., and Leibbrand, B. (2010) 'Nordic walking—trend or ideal performance training in breast cancer?' *Onkologie* 33(S6): 182–3.

Sprod, L. K., Drum, S. N., Bentz, A. T., Carter, S. D., and Schneider, C. M. (2005) 'The effects of walking poles on shoulder function in breast cancer survivors'. *Integrative Cancer Therapies* 4(4): 287–93.

Touillaud, M., Foucaut, A.-M., Berthouze, S. E., Reynes, E., Kempf-Lépine, A.-S., Carretier, J., Pérol, D., Guillemaut, S., Chabaud S., Bourne-Branchu, V., Perrier, L., Trédan, O., Fervers, B., and Bachmann, P. (2013) 'Design of a randomised controlled trial of adapted physical activity during adjuvant treatment for localised breast cancer: The PASAPAS feasibility study'. *BMJ Open* 3(10): e003855.

Menopause

Hagner, W., Hagner-Derengowska, M., Wiacek, M., and Zubrzycki, I. Z. (2009) 'Changes in level of VO2max, blood lipids, and waist circumference in the response to moderate endurance training as a function of ovarian aging'. *Menopause* 16(5): 1009–13.

Workplace health

Blasche, G., Pfeffer, M., Thaler, H., and Gollner, E. (2013) 'Work-site health promotion of frequent computer users: Comparing selected interventions'. *Work* 46(3): 233–41.

Fractured vertebrae

Wendlová, J. (2008) 'Nordic walking: Is it suitable for patients with fractured vertebra?' *Bratisl lek listy* 109(3): 171–6.

Various

Kapoor, S. (2013) 'Nordic walking and its clinical benefits in different disorders'. *Disabilities and Rehabilitation* 35(19): 1676.

RESEARCH ON HEALTHY SUBJECTS

Aigner, A., Ledl-Kurkowski, E., Hörl, S., and Salzmann K. (2004) 'Effects of Nordic walking and accordingly normal walking on heart rate and arterial lactate concentration'. *Austrian Journal of Sports Medicine* 3: 32–6.

Church, T. S., Earnest, C. P., and Morss, G. M. (2002) 'Field testing of physiological responses associated with Nordic walking'. *Research Quarterly of Exercise and Sport* 73(3): 296–300.

Hansen, E. A., and Smith, G. (2009) 'Energy expenditure and comfort during Nordic walking with different pole lengths'. *Journal of Strength and Conditioning Research* 23(4): 1187–94.

Jordan, A. N., Olson, T. P, Earnest, C. P., Morss, G. M., and Church, T. S. (2001) 'Metabolic cost of high intensity poling while Nordic walking versus normal walking'. *Medicine and Science in Sports and Exercise* 33(5S1): S86.

Jürimäe, T., Meema, K., Karelson, K., Purge, P., and Jürimäe, J. (2009) 'Intensity of Nordic walking in young females with different peak O2 consumption'. *Clinical Physiology and Functional Imaging* 29(5): 330–4.

Knobloch, K., and Vogt, P. M. (2006) '[Nordic pole walking injuries: Nordic walking thumb as novel injury entity]'. *Sportverletz Sportschaden* 20(3): 137–42.

Knobloch, K., Schreibmueller, L., Jagodzinski, M., Zeichen, J., and Krettek, C. (2007) 'Rapid rehabilitation programme following sacral stress fracture in a long-distance running female athlete'. *Archives of Orthopaedic and Trauma Surgery* 127(9): 809–13.

Knowles, A. M., Hill, J., Davies, H., Dancy, B., Mistry, N., Mellor, R., and Howatson, G. (2012) 'A pilot study examining the health benefits of Nordic walking in sedentary adults'. *Journal of Sport and Health Research* 4(1): 45–56.

Pérez-Soriano, P., Llana-Belloch, S., Martínez-Nova, A., Morey-Klapsing, G., and Encarnación-Martínez, A. (2011) 'Nordic walking practice might improve plantar pressure ditribution'. *Research Quarterly of Exercise and Sport* 82(4): 593–9.

Perrey, S., and Fabre, N. (2008) 'Exertion during uphill, level and downhill walking with or without hiking poles'. *Journal of Sports Science and Medicine* 7(1): 32–8.

Porcari, J. P., Hendrickson, T. L., Walter, P. R., Terry, L., and Walsko, G. (1997) 'The physiological responses to walking with and without Power Poles on treadmill exercise'. *Research Quarterly of Exercise and Sport* 68(2): 161–6.

Ripatti, T. (2002) 'Effect of Nordic Walking training program on cardiovascular fitness'. Academic degree study, Sportartspezifische Leistungsfähigkeit Deutsche Sporthochschule Köln, Germany.

Rodgers, C. D., VanHeest, J. L., and Schachter, C. L. (1995) 'Energy expenditure during submaximal walking with Exerstriders.' *Medicine and Science in Sports and Exercise* 27(4): 607–11.

Schiffer, T., Knicker, A., Hoffman, U., Harwig, B., Hollmann, W., and Struder, H. K. (2006) 'Physiological responses to Nordic walking, walking and jogging'. *European Journal of Applied Physiology* 98(1): 56–61.

Simic, M., Hinman, R. S., Wrigley, T. V., Bennell, K. L., and Hunt, M. A. (2011) 'Gait modification strategies for altering medial knee joint load: A systematic review'. *Arthritis Care and Research* 63(3): 405–26.

Sugiyama, K., Kawamura, M., Tomita, H., and Katamoto, S. (2013) 'Oxygen uptake, heart rate, perceived exertion, and integrated electromyogram of the lower and upper extremities during level and Nordic walking on a treadmill'. *Journal of Physiological Anthropology* 32: 2.

'Nordic Walking is an effective physical training modality in COPD. Functional exercise capacity was significantly increased and sustained over a *nine-month* test period. Uncomfortable feelings of breathlessness decreased and remained decreased.' (Breyer *et al.* 2010, emphasis added)

'Three months pole walking led to significant reduction in resting HR, diastolic and systolic blood pressure.' (Mikalacki *et al.* 2011)

'Numbers with depression significantly decreased following 24 weeks of Nordic walking. Mood was significantly elevated and motivation to exercise increased.' (Suija *et al.* 2009)

'Nordic walking intervention seems to decrease chemerin and leptin levels, and subjects in this intervention group achieved the most beneficial effects on components of MeS.

Improved lipid profile remained a predictor of decreased MetS score only in the Nordic walking group and it seems that Nordic walking has more beneficial effects on cardiovascular disease risks than RT [resistance training].' (Venojärvi *et al.* 2013)

'Nordic walking was superior to standard cardiac rehabilitation care in improving functional capacity and other important outcomes in patients with heart failure. This exercise modality is a promising alternative for this population.' (Keast *et al.* 2013)

'Nordic walking provided the best well-rounded benefits by improving upper-body strength, cardiovascular endurance, and flexibility. Therefore, Nordic walking is recommended as an effective and efficient mode of concurrent exercise to improve overall functional fitness in older adults.' (Takeshima 2013)

'NW led to short and medium term improvement of musculoskeletal complaints.' (Blasche *et al.* 2013)

'Compared to regular walking, Nordic walking, examined in the field, results in a significant increase in oxygen use and caloric expenditure compared to regular walking, without significantly increasing perceived exertion.' (Church *et al.* 2002)

'In conclusion, pulmonary rehabilitation with a Nordic walking program is a safe and feasible physical activity in end-stage lung disease patients referred for lung transplantation and results in improvements in patients' mobility and quality of life.' (Jastrzebski D *et al.* 2013)

PART SEVEN 7

WANT TO KNOW

A HISTORY AND THE WORLDWIDE SCENE

20

Nordic walking has probably been around since people started to race on the skis they used as a means of transport in the winter. Cross-country skiing is a major pastime in all skiing nations, especially in Europe, and ski poles are used extensively to propel the skier forwards (and uphill). It stands to reason that keen racers would replicate this action during the summer without the skis, when there was no snow on the ground. It is widely believed that this was common practice in parts of Scandinavia as early as the 1930s.

Nordic walking enthusiasts argue continually about who invented the sport and how it should be done. Lots of ideas and theories have contributed to a mix of techniques that suit an equally unlimited mix of needs and preferences. At NWUK, for instance we tend to concentrate more on the individual than the technique, and just ensure that the poles provide maximum results, progression and fun. The four-gear technique steps outlined in this book are derived from my experiences when teaching ordinary everyday people from a variety of backgrounds. I do not regard myself at all as a 'technical' expert – I just have a good understanding of the variations of technique and how to help people get *results*.

THE DEVELOPMENT OF NORDIC WALKING

Here's a brief overview of how Nordic walking in its present form is believed to have come into being.

1960s–90s

A Finnish PE teacher and university lecturer is said to have introduced the summer version of cross-country skiing into her lessons as early as 1966 and even showcased it on national Finnish TV. Despite this, there is little evidence of any formalised approach of this aspect of pole walking until about 1997.

In the US, an innovative fitness enthusiast called Tom Rutlin was also experimenting with pole walking and embarking on a one-man crusade to develop his own unique technique, teaching method and poles (Exerstrider). Tom called it 'pole walking' and his method does differ from that derived from the use of ski poles (see pages 27–28).

In 1997, Exel Oy, a Finnish pole manufacturer, introduced the first fitness-specific walking pole, based on the cross-country ski simulation method. Exel also supported research to develop and launch the activity on a more commercial basis. Marko Kanteneva and Risto Kasurinen, two Finns credited with creating and promoting the activity, were based at the Finnish Institute of Sport. They were integral to the drive to develop the more structured format for Nordic walking that still forms the basis of what we see in many countries today.

Nordic walking grew most rapidly in countries like Germany, Austria and Finland, although small pockets of walkers appeared in other nations, too. It was generally retail-led – that is, promoted by equipment manufacturers – and there was no formalised structure, so as pioneers tried to launch the sport in their respective countries a number of different variations and methods emerged. In Germany alone there were (and still are) several different training organisations, and as you can see from Figure 20.1 (page 183), this is also the case in several other countries.

In 2000, Aki Karihtala, the former president of Exel Oy, was integral to the formation of the International Nordic Walking Association (INWA). While this small committee made an attempt at standardising the sport, it may simply have been a case of shutting the stable door after the horse had bolted.

At the time when NWUK were the INWA's UK representatives (see below), it had become apparent that many member countries had already established different teaching methods and learning criteria. In many cases, the concentration was so focused on 'methods' and 'technique' that insufficient attention was being paid to the need for instructors to understand how to safely apply the principles of fitness and to understand how people actually learned new skills. It was evident that many potential Nordic walkers were put off by strict technique teaching. For the sport to become popular more attention to ability and results was the key.

Here are some of the methods of pole walking that evolved over time:
- The (ALFA) technique (International Nordic fitness association; INFO).
- The American Nordic Walking Association (ANWA) method.
- The INWA method.
- The Exerstrider method (Tom Rutlin; see Chapter 2).
- The NWUK four 'gears' outlined in this book.

Fundamental differences usually centre around the following:
- Whether the arm is kept straight on the forward arm swing or bent at the elbow (and what degree).
- Whether the pole is 'thrown away' on the back swing or control retained via a light grip.
- Whether rotation of the upper body is emphasised as a teaching point or encouraged to improve naturally.
- Length of stride and required pole length.

These variations and the lack of cohesion meant that those wishing to promote the activity most effectively in their respective nations were faced with a number of factors when developing their own processes:
1. What technique or method to adopt in order to get results.
2. What teaching processes and standards were required.
3. How to align these to the current educational criteria required in the individual country (qualification credit framework).

4. How to support those they trained to ensure they would succeed.

2001–10

Nordic walking was growing in popularity in countries across the world (see below for examples). In the UK, Martin Christie and Francis Mitchell set up the first instructor training workshops in 2004, initially using the INWA method.

During this period a number of the methods/organisations outlined above made a bid for 'international status' and the original INWA became the Nordic Walking Federation (although still known as INWA). They also launched an updated method: the '10-step technique', originally devised by Malin Svensson, a Nordic walking expert from the US. However, to date, no single organisation represents more than a small percentage of the instructors who operate around the world and there is still no instructor training method that is truly internationally recognised other than by the body who created it (although there is now an externally assessed qualification created by NWUK that is recognised by the Register of Exercise Professionals in many countries – see below).

2010–12

Having teamed up with Exercise Anywhere (a fitness industry consultancy), Martin Christie joined myself and a team of professional tutors. The team are Nicky Parsons, Tanya Adolpho, Jason Feavers, Trish Cowie and Dawn Mclean, all of whom have been integral to the development of much of the content in this book and have also created a number of additional CPD (continuing professional development points) training modules such as well-being, weight loss and ski fit. The team have trained in excess of 2,500 instructors and supported over 200 community and well-being projects.

Martin and the NWUK team went on to develop:

- The first formal vocational qualification based solely on fitness and Nordic walking. The CYQ Certificate in Fitness Walking is a Level 2 fitness qualification mapped to fitness industry standards and the UK qualification credit framework. It provides entry to REPs (the Register of Exercise Professionals: www.exerciseregister.org) or in Europe eREPS (www.ereps.eu.com), is externally assessed and now being adopted by other training organisations.

- A diploma in exercise referral that can be delivered outdoors with Nordic walking as the key exercise component.

Martin Christie on the creation of the CYQ formal qualification

'The philosophy was simple … we would never put a beginner on a cross-trainer machine in the gym and expect them to immediately be able to master the top setting but with many technique-centred Nordic walking training methods, that was the case. We wanted to create highly skilled instructors who could match technique with ability, add progression and get results.

'We also wanted this form of fitness to be recognised as worthy of a specific fitness instruction qualification.'

NWUK has also trained instructors who now operate in a number of other countries, including Norway, Greece, Israel, Dubai, France, Switzerland, Cyprus, Portugal, Spain, Netherlands, Malta and Singapore. More recently, together with other leading organisations they have formed the World Nordic Walking Alliance.

Many other significant training organisations have also found it necessary to align their training with the education establishments of their own nation in order to gain credibility with both the medical fraternity and fitness industry. This more rounded approach ensures that instructors have the skills to understand and adapt technique according to the fitness level and mobility of the client.

During the development of the teaching processes in the UK, NWUK have liaised directly with many of the leading and most successful training organisations in other countries, many of which embrace a range of techniques and bring in a range of skills from other industries. Some of them have kindly agreed to contribute to this book with an outline of what they deliver and why.

AUSTRALIA

Mike Gates is the founder of Poleabout in Australia. Since 2001 he has worked alongside some of the original Finnish experts and developed an in-depth understanding of most elements of technique. Interestingly, while he started out using only strapped Nordic walking poles, he is now also an advocate of the Exerstrider strapless poles. He has a generally relaxed attitude to technique and even pole height adjustments, and yet a serious and highly skilful attitude to helping people to achieve their goals.

Mike has trained over 1,000 instructors and leaders in Australia, and his inspirational attitude

Mike Gates on Nordic walking

'I had the great privilege to learn the strap method of the Finnish way of Nordic walking in the spring of 2001 and implemented the training processes on this style of walking with poles for nearly a decade. Then, in early 2010 I had the grand opportunity to meet up and learn from another modern-day pole-walking legend, Tom Rutlin from the USA, whose style utilises the strapless method of walking with poles. And for more than three and a half years now I have integrated and adapted both strap and strapless styles of walking with poles into our education and training programme to suit the multiple needs and health/fitness and recreational requirements of the general public – as one style/method or size does not suit/fit all within our communities in Australia.

'When it comes to pole sizing, I have a much more flexible approach and use two formulas as a baseline to start from. The other deciding factors that should go into selecting pole length are the individual's natural body mobility and stability and their ability at the introductory set-up. These should then be revisited frequently as those three factors will, over time with regular use, improve. In short I believe that no one formula fits all. My mantra is: "get on your poles and off your pills for a better way of life"'

to pole walking is infectious. He also passionately believes that all instructors should have basic fitness industry qualifications. When he visited the UK in 2011 he wowed our instructors with his use of Exerstrider poles, which clearly showed his depth of knowledge. His version of pole walking was quick to learn and effective, but had elements that reflected both Exerstrider and the angled pole plant that comes from the traditional Nordic walking styles.

SPAIN

Other experts that I have met have a less relaxed attitude to technique or pole height adjustment, and yet they are still open to adaptation and evolution. Their achievements in their respective countries are no less remarkable. José Manuel Fernández Molina is the author of a Spanish language technique book titled *Caminar Nordico con Bastiones* and founder of the Escuela Espanola de Nordic walking. He has trained over 500 instructors since 2007, and they are required to complete 8 hours of pre-learning, 2 days of practical tuition and 10 hours of practice. José and his team also work extensively with those suffering from ill health, and he has created a number of DVDs. José is a skilled practitioner and he describes his technique sequence as having four key elements:

José Manuel Fernández Molina

'I am ready to explore all methods and personally do not think there is a right or wrong technique – I like to just like to ensure the method being taught is actually possible.

'Our team consists of an international Nordic walking coach, a therapist and licensed physical education specialists in sports medicine. We have developed a methodology framed within science and efficiency along with the experience of over 30 years in the world of sport and physical activity.

'Nordic walking poles must provide two factors essential for good practice: comfort in their use and effectiveness in the course of a walk. The length of poles varies according to the height of the walker but for guidance we advise that the pole be about 70 per cent of the user's height as a starting point. This means the walker should simply multiply his/her height by 0.7. For example, a walker 1.80m tall would require a pole of 1.26m:

$$1.80m \times 0.7 = 1.26m$$

The formula can vary according to the intensity of the training though, and speed is important too. In Nordic walking it is the force exerted on the poles that determines the cadence (speed). The faster you walk, the more likely it is that you no longer walk with the proper stride length. Gathering speed often means a loss of technique because the control is no longer with the poles but has been passed back to the legs. That is *not* Nordic walking but "race walking" with poles.

'In studies conducted by our instructors, they determined the approximate maximum speed per kilometre at which good technique was lost. It is very important to note that the instructors varied in height and step length is closely linked to the stature of the instructor. The height of the instructors used in the trials were: 1.70m and 1.76m.

'The measurements were carried out at distances of 10, 15, 20 and 48km. Our findings were that the maximum speed at which correct execution of technique is not lost (technical Nordic walking) was between 6.30 and 7 minutes per km.'

- A high pole position.
- Arms kept wide (with a soft bend at the elbow but not crossing the body).
- Releasing the pole in a triangle.
- Wide stride and good foot action.

José also embraces strapless poles and even a type of pole with a built-in suspension system.

ITALY

Nordic walking is very popular in Italy and there is huge interest both in urban and rural areas. Fabio Moretti is the founder of the Scuola Italiana Nordic Walking, which has trained 2,100 instructors since 2008. Fabio is a former ski coach and athlete with a passion for well-being, and his instructor training requires the learner to undergo 10 hours of technique training before attending

Fabio Moretti on Nordic walking

'We teach Nordic walking technique with the "push away" method, but it's different from the other techniques because they complete the push away with an intra-rotation of the wrist and a rigid position of upper body, which is a very unnatural movement. Instead we push away with a natural movement of the hand (push on the wrist straps), with the hand parallel to the pole.

'In this way we can obtain more involvement of the back, but at the same time more involvement of lower body, because the leg movement is wider.

'We made some studies with modified Nordic walking poles (with a loading cell mounted on top of them) and it was clear that the method engaged the abdominal muscles far more significantly than normal walking. We measured it to be at least 10 times more than walking without poles.

'We have defined our method of *metodo delle 5 fasi*. In English it would probably be the "five phases method" or "five steps method". The steps are:
1. Relaxing and recovery of natural walking.
2. Coordinating development and alternate technique.
3. Postural elements.
4. Breathing elements.
5. Advanced techniques.

'The first two steps are the core of the teaching method because they work on the recovery of natural and correct walking without poles, which is essential to the next step of developing an alternate technique with the use of the poles as a natural consequence. In the second step we work on a series of coordinated exercises to develop the correct use of the pole to obtain a little wider movement of the legs and arms (our unique characteristic). The third step involves some tips and exercises (particularly concerning the back, shoulder and hips) to obtain a better posture and movement. The fourth step involves a series of exercises to use correct breathing with and without poles, and explains the benefits we can obtain from it. In the fifth step we combine other exercises and movements that can be used to obtain a complete workout with Nordic walking, for example sports technique, warm-up and cool-down exercises, circuit training coordination/strength/stretching exercises, games with poles, and so on'.

two 2-day practical courses. He also has modules for dealing with medical conditions like diabetes and hypertension. Fabio operates up to 15 classes a week in Rome and up to 100 people Nordic walk as a group at any one time.

He advocates a fairly strict technique that does include the push away (on the back swing) and the very straight arm on the front swing seen in many European methods, but he is keen to point out that he has adapted this to a more natural form that does not involve all the characteristics usually found in these methods.

TOM RUTLIN AND THE EXERSTRIDER TECHNIQUE

Tom Rutlin continues to promote his methods around the world and now has over 2,000 instructors using his method. I have included a section of Exerstrider technique in Tom's own words, on pages 27–28 of this book, but he outlines his concept below:

'My aim in developing my Exerstride method of Nordic walking was, first of all, to *not* mess with the natural walking gait mechanics that are programmed into all human DNA, and then to maximise the physiological impact of adding specially designed poles against which force is applied, thus engaging as much muscle mass as possible. My aim was to create a total-body version of walking that could benefit people of all ages, abilities and health and fitness goals.

'All forms and techniques are hybrids of walking and Nordic skiing. Among the earliest versions in the fitness walking with poles/Nordic walking genealogy are Exerstriding (a means of simultaneously exercising all the body's major muscles as one strides, walks, runs, skips or bounds), in which natural walking has provided

the dominant gene, and Nordic skiing techniques have been altered to maximise the work of core and upper body muscles. Another is Sauvekeavely (pole walking), in which the dominant feature is derived from skiing. The gait and sporting ethos of this early root of Nordic walking more closely resembles the stride of skiing than it does natural walking.

'The former is a physical activity intended to tune the body, and promote health and safe, functional movement. The Finnish roots of Nordic walking had a sport paradigm designed to train the body for improved athletic performance.

'The many other popular forms of Nordic walking that have emerged over the years are hybrids of the original physical activity and sport hybrids. I continue to believe that only by offering to those we hope to attract to Nordic walking competent instruction in all time-tested and researched methods of Nordic walking will the Nordic walking movement ever reach its unlimited full potential to both change lives and add enjoyment.'

NORDIC WALKING AROUND THE WORLD

There are a number of other experts, pioneers and dedicated Nordic walking professionals around the world. For readers with a keen interest in gathering a balanced view of Nordic walking techniques there are publications available by the following authors which will provide an in-depth evaluation: Suzanne Nottingham (and Alexandra Jurasin), Malin Svensson, Klaus Swanbeck, Andreas Willhelm and José Manuel Fernández Molina.

Figure 20.1 illustrates the spread of Nordic walking national organisations around the world by 2013. My research of these shows that in many instances no structured delivery processes

UK	www.nordicwalking.co.uk www.britishnordicwalking.org.uk	**France**	www.marchenordiquefrance. blogspot.co.uk www.fnsmr.org
Spain	http//escuelaespañoladenordic walking.com www.nordicwalkinginwafederacion. blogspot.co.uk www.nordicfitness.net	**Canada**	www.urbanpoling.com www.nordixx.com
Italy	www.scuolaitaliananordicwalking.it www.nordicwalkingacademy.it www.anwi.it	**Australia**	www.polewalkabout.com www.nordicwalkingaustralia.com.au www.nordicacademy.com.au
Germany	www.nordic-walking-union.de/ nordic-walking www.nordicfitness.net	**New Zealand**	www.nordicwalkingnz.co.nz www.nordicwalking.net.nz
Switzerland	www.swissnordicfitness.ch	**Israel**	www.ecologym.net
Taiwan	pfchen51@gmail.com	**Netherlands**	www.nordicwalking.nl
USA	www.walkingpoles.com www.nordicwalknow.com www.anwa.us www.nordicwalkingna.com	**Poland**	www.pfnw.eu
		Slovenia	www.znhs.si
		Estonia	www.kepikond.ee
		Belgium	www.nordicwalking.be
		Japan	http://jnfa.jp

Figure 20.1 Nordic walking organisations worldwide

are yet in place either due to the fact that Nordic walking is still in its infancy in that country or that enthusiasts rather than experienced training bodies are trying to get it established.

I think it also provides a clear picture that there is no dominant technique, method or organisation, and that perhaps it would be more prudent to draw on the collective expertise of all of those who are successfully delivering Nordic walking rather than attempt to establish one. It would benefit Nordic walking if there was more focus on ensuring that instructors are equipped with the necessary skills to really engage with the population and inspire them to take up Nordic walking for life.

I understand that Nordic walking takes place in the following countries but found no specific website information about teaching organisations: Latvia, China, Hungary, India, Austria, Greece, Norway, Finland, UAE, Cyprus, Malta.

NORDIC WALKING PARKS AND FESTIVALS

One aspect of Nordic walking that has huge potential all over the world is the creation of Nordic walking parks. These can be as comprehensive as ski resorts, with graded 'runs' which Nordic walkers can tackle all year round (weather permitting). Mainly in tourist areas of

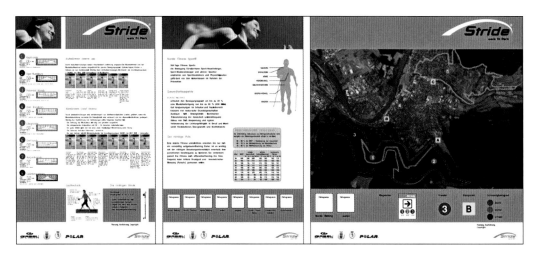

Figure 20.2 A guide to the routes in a Nordic walking park

outstanding natural beauty and areas where skiing is prolific, they provide a perfect visitor attraction in the months when there is no snow. Some have pole hire facilities, and even gates to time the walker from start to finish, and others come with route guides (such as the one in Figure 20.2) to help the walker select the route according to distance, gradient and degree of difficulty.

The parks are carefully planned and use professional GPS devices from leading GIS survey companies. Gianpietro Beltramello from Gabel srl (a leading Italian pole manufacturer) has been involved with the creation of seven 'Stride walk-fit parks' worldwide, and he uses digital land models to supplement the GPs information in order to accurately calculate elevation profiles, time calculations and the determination of difficulties. The process of development is complex, and also involves aerial photography, detailed maps and assessment of signage and safety. Consideration is also given to how the routes, which can cover up to 50km, can be used by Nordic skiers, bladers, hikers, snowshoers and even mountain bikers.

Not all parks are in mountains or country parks, and the potential to create fantastic outdoor areas where well-being is the main focus is a growing trend, perfect for more urban areas. These parks provide people with the opportunity to enjoy being active with an element of measurement and progression. They can be enjoyed by solitary walkers, for exercise prescription and rehabilitation groups, or simply for social groups. For effectiveness, it is essential to also provide tuition and some form of control mechanism to establish ability and health screening prior to use. In the UK the NWUK Freedom Card is designed for this purpose, and the first Nordic walking park in the UK was opened in October 2013. While only on a fairly small scale, this concept at High Woods Country Park in Colchester, Essex was the brainchild of NWUK instructor Penny Parker, supported by her local council. There are way-marked routes, and people are encouraged to enjoy the routes in instructed sessions or on their own. Plans for pole hire and further developments are in hand.

TAKING IT FURTHER

21

Having read this book, you will hopefully become a Nordic walker for life so at NWUK we have created an online resource section to ensure you can access regularly updated workout plans, events and races and even find out more about associated sports and activities. See below for a couple of sample workout plans and a brief list of associated sports.

SAMPLE WORKOUT PLANS

These are examples of the downloadable one-hour workout walk ideas that involve Nordic walking poles and techniques. They are all easy to memorise and give a good guide to how you can pep up your own Nordic walks by using the four-gear system, the principles of intensity, and simple, effective additional exercises along the way. They can be used to accelerate weight loss, train for an event or simply target problem areas like the backs of arms or the backside. Your local instructor will use similar methods to help you to get the results you want. For more downloadable workout plans visit www.nordicwalking.co.uk/completeguide

NO 'BUTTS' WORKOUT PLAN

This is a no-excuses workout walk that adds extra work for the legs and backside. Ideally choose a location where you have access to a fairly steep bank or hill to tackle and a flatter area for the drills immediately below. In this workout there are three key phases to remember:

* Phase 1 'Triple-2' hill drills − 3 × 2 minute hill drills
* Phase 2 Interval sequences − 2 × 5 minute interval sequences that are simple to remember (skip, lunge, walk and skate, squat, walk), all are repeated
* Phase 3 − repeat of the hill drills sequence above.

Action	Time in minutes	Notes	Progression
Warm up	5	Dynamic warm-up	
Nordic walk in Gear 1	2	Usual pace	
Nordic walk in Gear 2	3	Usual pace	
Nordic walk in Gear 3	4	Brisk pace	
Triple-2 hillwork			
Walk uphill with no poles	2	Take quite large slow steps	Locate a steeper hill or increase drills by 30 seconds every two workouts
Walk downhill with no poles	2	Take care not to slip – keep weight on heels and knees bent	
Walk up and down with poles	2	Faster pace – keep weight on heels and knees bent as above on downhill	Push off from toes on uphill to engage buttocks more on uphill
1-1-3 drill sequence 1 (skip, lunge, walk)			
Skip (on level surface) with poles	1		Increase to 2 minutes and add 30 seconds every second workout
Slow down, stop and perform 10 Lunge steps with double poling	1	Perform them slowly and carefully	Add five repetitions every second workout and perform without poles once confident
Nordic walk through the gears to maintain Gear 3	3	Brisk pace	
1-1-3 drill sequence 2 (skate, squat, walk)			
Skating drill	1	See page 119 for technique	Increase to 2 minutes and add 30 seconds every second workout
Slow down, stop and perform 10 squats using poles for support	1	Perform them slowly and carefully	Add five repetitions every second workout and perform without poles once confident
Nordic walk through the gears to maintain Gear 3	3	Brisk pace	
Repeat drill sequences 1 and 2	10		
Repeat triple-2 hillwork	6		
Nordic walk through the gears to Gear 3	4		
Nordic walk in Gear 2	3	Usual pace	
Nordic walk in Gear 1	2	Usual pace	
Cool down and stretch	5		

Table 21.1 No 'butts' workout plan

WEIGHT LOSS WORKOUT

This workout is based on basic principles that help to accelerate weight loss: the simple calorie-burning effect of using major muscles effectively with the boost of tempo variations and simple resistance drills. Technique and speed are utilised here in order to really engage your muscles and cardiovascular system, and you can choose how to incorporate resistance depending on where you are and who you are with. Do not over-stride or go too fast, watching technique at all times. Also, remember to use your rate of perceived exertion (RPE) scale (see page 126) – this way you will gain more from the workout and can progress more effectively. To help you remember the sequence I have built it into a simple set of three 3-minute speed and tech drills followed by alternate upper and lower-body resistance work.

Action	Time in minutes	Notes	Progression
Warm up	5	Dynamic warm up	
Nordic walk in Gear 1	1	Steady pace	
Nordic walk in Gear 2	2	Steady pace	
Nordic walk in Gear 3	2	Steady pace but drop to 2 if struggling to maintain technique	
Triple-3 sequence			
Nordic walk in Gear 2	3	Fast pace – drop pace if struggling to maintain technique	Add 30 seconds every second workout
Nordic walk in Gear 3	3	Brisk pace but drop to 2 if struggling to maintain technique	
Nordic walk in Gear 2	3	Fast pace – drop pace if struggling to maintain technique	Add 30 seconds every second workout
10 × upper body resistance exercises (choose from band, partner or street furniture – see page 128)	1	Perform the exercises slowly and with full, good technique	Add 5 more repetitions every third workout
Repeat triple-3 sequence	9		
10 × lower body resistance exercises (choose from squat or lunge – see pages 129–130)		Perform the exercises slowly and with full, good technique	Add 5 more repetitions every third workout
Repeat triple-3 sequence	9		
Repeat 10 × upper body resistance	1		
Repeat triple-3 sequence	9		
Repeat 10 × lower body resistance			
Nordic walk in Gear 3	2	Steady pace but drop to 2 if struggling to maintain technique	
Nordic walk in Gear 2	2	Steady pace	
Nordic walk in Gear 1	1	Steady pace	
Cool down and stretch	5		

Table 21.2 Weight loss workout

TRYING OTHER NORDIC SPORTS

If Nordic walking has inspired you to take up other forms of Nordic sports – here is a brief run through of other sports that involve the poles, similar movements and terrain and how you can have a go.

CROSS-COUNTRY SKIING

Using many of the same basic movements as outlined in the book but with a larger range of movement, cross-country skiing is the perfect way to explore true winter wonderlands without the need for a ski lift. For more information see:

- www.tracks-and-trails.com
- www.basi.org.uk/content/nordic.aspx

SNOWSHOEING

Originally used by trappers and traders as a way to move about in deep snow, snowshoeing is now used primarily as recreation. The aim is to spread your weight and not accumulate snow so you can travel across stunning landscapes that would usually be impossible to walk on – poles provide stability and indicate snow depth. For more information see:

- www.mountainpassions.com/winter_ski/ winter_activities/snowshoe_beginners_guide. html
- www.tracks-and-trails.com

NORDIC BLADING OR ROLLER SKIING

Like Nordic walking, this type of roller blading on long ski-like skates originated as a summer training regime for cross-country skiers. It is now also a sport in its own right and there are championships and events. For more information see:

- www.roller-skis.com
- www.abc-of-skiing.com/rollerskiing.asp

Figure 21.1 Cross-country skiing and Nordic blading

TAKING PART IN EVENTS AND CHALLENGES

There are now many designated Nordic walking challenges and both trail and road marathons are beginning to welcome Nordic walkers too. NWUK hosts regional adventure walks and coordinates weekend breaks, festivals and holidays. There are also a number of personal challenges that you can undertake, either as a part of a charity trek or by ticking off some of the long distance paths or iconic routes such as the Inca trail. For a comprehensive list of events that welcome Nordic Walkers and ideas for personal or charity challenges visit www.nordicwalking.co.uk/completeguide

INDEX